AMERICAN JUSTICE SYSTEM UNCOVERED

TABLE OF CONTENTS

	PAGES
The Author	3
Foreword	5
Acknowledgement	7
Introduction	9
Systematic Cronyism	16
The Great Deceivers	56
Judicial Terrorist	59
Extortion of Children	60
Systematic Disenfranching Minority Youth	61
Business of the Justice System	68
Unpublished Judgment	71
Systematic Racism	91
Government Conspiracy Theory	103
U.S. Knowledge of Drug Trafficking	111
Government Endorsed Addiction	124
Cocaine A Major Player In U.S. History	126
American Terrorism	130
Black Wall Street	133
Louisiana Small Claims Court (A Façade)	137

Now Into Court	152
Systematic Elimination of Black Farmers	180
Reparation For Slavery	192
Sowing And Reaping (Terrorism)	212
Hopeless People Are Dangerous People	220
Community Policing	228
Conclusion	231

THE AUTHOR

Rev. Donald Britton was born in a very small rural area of West Monroe, Louisiana. He attended from first to the twelfth grade a small school Central High School where he graduated in 1969. The total population of the school was 267 students. Although the school was small the student received a quality education. Most students upon graduation were ready for employment in areas such as animal husbandry, agriculture, carpentry and many others fields. After a tour in the U.S. Army where he got married and later divorced; Rev. Britton was lead to further his education.

He studied legal studies and theology at two schools at the same time, United Theology Seminary and Northeast Louisiana University. He received a Bachelor of Art in Legal Studies and a Bachelor of Theology. His original intent was to pursue a law degree but soon found his passion was for ministry. Rev. Britton returned to college while working as police officer and received a Master of Arts in Mental Health Counseling and became a Licensed Addiction Counselor and A Certified Clinical Chaplain.

Rev. Britton has worked with the juvenile population for years as a Boy Scout Master, Bible teacher and motivational speaker. Rev. Britton received the nomination of Outstanding Young Men of America in 1984. He is a member of the Society of Author Composers and Publisher. He has also done extensive work with the HIV/AIDS population as a counselor and tester.

He is the proud father of Duchess I. Britton an educator and graduate of Grambling State University (Summa Cum Laude) with a Master of Education Degree. Casino R. Britton graduate of Grambling State University with a Bachelor Degree in Criminal Justice. Antonio D. Britton a graduate of Embry Riddle

Aeronautical University with a Master of Aeronautical Engineering Degree.

Find a comfortable place, relax and read American Justice System Uncovered. It will bring you to a totally new awareness of our justice system.

FOREWORD

The recent killings of young black males by white cops have again brought to the forefront issues and problems pertaining to race and justice in America. The killing of Michael Brown by police officer Darren Wilson in Ferguson, Missouri, and the killing of Eric Garner by police officer Daniel Pantaleo in Staten Island, New York, resulted in public outrage, widespread protests, and calls for changes in the methods and practices of policing in America, especially in low income black urban communities. The main issue and problem centered on a pattern of reckless, unwarranted, and excessive use of lethal force by white police officers that resulted in the killing of unarmed young black males by white police officers, and the failure to indict or prosecute the police officers who committed these act in the face of clear and compelling evidence. The raised hands of Michael Brown and the desperate uttering of "I can't breathe" by Eric Garner have been used as rallying calls for racial justice in policing by millions of people across the nation.

Despite the intricacies involved in the criminal justice system, in general, and policing, in specific, the pattern of using deadly force by white police officers against black males is not only disturbing, and an indictment of the criminal justice system, but also calls into question the quality of justice by the criminal justice system. These incidents also reveal that there are serious problems pertaining to race and justice in America. The author of "Louisiana Justice System Uncovered," illustrates that the problems in the criminal justice system in Louisiana and the nation are chronic and systemic and run deeper than the police, but also extends into the prosecution, the court, the penal system, and the correctional system.

The author of this book documents with observations, personal experiences, and public records that the criminal justice system is not "blind" to race, gender, social class, economic status, social connections, place of residence and reputation of the defendant, the accuser, or the witnesses. Nor is the criminal justice system blind to the race, gender, and social status of the police, prosecutors, judges, jurors, or correctional officers and that discretionary justice often leads to injustice. In "American Justice System Uncovered" the author not only provides knowledge of the problems in the criminal justice system, but also serves as a source of motivation for public dialogue on solutions to problems in our system of justice or otherwise the need for reform and social change.

Thomas J. Durant, Jr., Ph.D.

Emeritus Professor of Criminology

ACKNOWLEDGE

To all of the good law enforcement officers who put their lives on the line every day to keep our cities, towns, villages, hamlets and states safe, this book is written in honor of you.

To all of the good judges who preside over courts and put aside all of your personal ambitions, prejudices and bias so that justices may prevail, this book is written in honor of you.

To all of the good lawyers who place fairness and honesty above their bank accounts; this book was written in honor of you.

Ironically I must thank all of the racist, bigots and corrupt judges. Many who are written about in this book who wear the robe daily in disgrace to the American System of Justice. Had it not been for you I would have never found the motivation to write this book.

To all of the military men and women who go to war risking life and limbs for the cause of freedom this book is dedicated to you.

To all of the Black men who fought in wars for America for freedom that they themselves did not have; this book is dedicated to you.

A special thanks to my friend Eva Harris for her assistance in the publication of this book.

My thanks and sincere gratitude to Dr. Thomas Durant, Ph.D for taking time from his busy schedule to do the foreword for my book.

INTRODUCTION

"Why do you show me iniquity and cause me to behold grievance? For spoiling and violence are before me: and there are they that raise up strife and contention. Therefore the law is slacked, and judgment doth never go forth: for the wicked doth compass about the righteous; therefore wrong judgment proceedeth. This quote was written by a Biblical prophet in the bible (Habakkuk 1:2-4). He saw then what I see now in our judicial system. My daily prayer is that this country will not have to learn the same lesson as the Judean people that Habakkuk wrote about.

On yesterday I arose early to go to the court house to check on some business that was pending. It was one of those days where you had to drive for ten or fifteen minutes to find a parking space. The court house is usually one of the busiest places in Baton Rouge. After finding a parking space about a block away, I began my walk to the court house in the cold weather breeze. In the distance I saw a Black man walking with two signs. I strained my eyes to trying to read the signs from a half block away but I could not. After crossing the street I approached him and began to read the signs. He was carrying one sign in each hand. One of the signs read "my boss says a monkey can do my job." Another sentence read, "my boss says all Black men need to be in prison." I observed another picture on the sign of a hangman rope hanging over a pipe and the writing under it saying "this rope was placed in the employee locker room." I asked him why was he carry those signs and who was his boss. He told me that he was advised not to disclose the name of his boss or call any names. I told him if these statements on the sign are true that I would print all of their names on the sign. But he was hesitant about printing the adversaries' names on the picket sign. I will not use his name because I did not ask his permission to do so.

This man had been walking around the court house for weeks protesting the injustices and racism he had received on a Louisiana state job. He told me that he had spent all of his money on lawyers and had not accomplished anything. EEOC had given him a right to sue letter of authorization, but the judge maneuvered around the right to sue letter stating that the time to file his suit was prescribed or simply speaking he didn't file it in time. He told me that one of the attorneys that he had gone to had promised to take the case only to hold the file one day before the deadline to file the suit. Now he is without a job, no income, and spends most of his day marching the street with his sign protesting the injustices done to him. It saddens me as I walked away thinking of how many time I have seen these evil injustices placed upon people in my community. These injustices are done because of a racist and corrupt legal system which allows attorneys to do these things with impunity.

    I have discovered in my sixty three years upon this earth that everything has a purpose and there is a purpose for everything; nothing in this life happens in a vacuum. Even the bad things can be used to give one a better quality of life. If a poisonous snake bites you. I doubt that you will find it beneficial at the present moment. But the irony of the snake bite is that if you are ever bitten again the venom will be much less harmful to your body simply because you would have built up immunity to the snake's venom. I have tasted the venom of the Louisiana so called "justice system" and it has made me a more informed and stronger person as a result. I have been a victim of the so-called justice system and have seen countless others lives ruined by racist judges who bring their bigotry and racism to the bench on a daily basis. I have also seen how the poor and minorities are abused and robbed by the court systems especially Black men and frequently by Black judges. After being wrongfully charged with theft twice. Once for a dental bill because I refused to pay a dentist for his incompetent dental work; and again several years later being charged with theft from a mental client at a mental facility where I was the director. I began to wonder how many people in this state and country are sitting in prisons because they are poor, a minority, or Black. This is why I have taken the time from my very busy schedule to uncover and show you the real story behind the American Court Systems.

When I began thinking about a title for this book at first I considered many titles but after much prayer God gave me the title of American Justice System Uncovered. I took a long look at the O.J. Simpson trial and how hypocritical the legal system can be. O.J. Simpson was found not guilty of a crime that he more than likely committed and prosecuted and sentenced to prison for a crime that he obviously had nothing to do with (armed robbery of his own property).

I heard a preacher once say that if life gives you sour lemons make some lemonade. Life is filled with swift transitions. Today you are happy and tomorrow you're sad. Last year you were rich this year you may be poor. We live vicarious lives through our automobiles, homes, children, associations and affiliations. So much of our time is spent trying to find happiness and it's all right between our ears.

I ask myself this question often, "what do you see?" Do you see life obstruction as larger than life or do you see each day with a challenge that will enhance your growth as a person? If you see life's road blocks and pit falls as simply a challenge that you must overcome; then much of your daily stress will be eliminated in the process. Challenges are tools that our Creator uses to build many wonderful things in his people's lives, such as integrity, patience, hope, character, faith and endurance. These are the thing that one should long to hand down to his children more than the materialistic things that last only for a season.

In America we have many freedoms. Because of the vast freedoms we have we also have one the world's largest prison systems. The United States of America incarcerates over two million three hundred thousand peoples in prisons throughout the country. One of the greatest ironies is that over ninety percent of the people incarcerated are there due to a plea bargain. By that I mean that the person incarcerated seldom is tried on the charge for which they were arrested. The District Attorney sometimes systematically intimidates and threatens them with long harsh sentences if they do not plead guilty to a lesser charge. In actuality many of them are not guilty of any charge but rather than risk being sent to prison for a long period of time, they opt out by pleading guilty to a lesser charge. When one looks at the ratio to the proportion of the population the vast majority of these are Blacks, African Americans and racial minority groups. It makes you wonder why so many African Americans and racial minorities are in prisons? Is it that they just don't get it, are they just people who are genetically predisposed to be criminals? Are they a people who are cursed to be a sub servant group of people?

For an individual to be functional and productive in society, there are certain thing he/she must understand about themselves, who they are and their purpose in life.

The human being has three types of needs that must be fulfilled to be a healthy person. These needs are philosophical, psychological and spiritual; better known as soul, body and spirit or the trinity of the human. If any of these areas of a person's life are not fulfilled that person will have an emptiness or a void and will become a dysfunctional individual. They will not be able to attain their purpose in life to the fullest extent. The individual in an attempt to fill the void or emptiness may resort to the use of drugs, alcohol, sexual promiscuity, compulsive work habits, compulsive behavior disorders, overeating and a variety of other unhealthy behaviors because of a void in his or her life.

If one does not know the purpose of a thing they will eventually abuse that thing. Try giving a baby an unfamiliar object to play with. The child will examine the object for a while and if he/she does not soon figure out what to do with it the next activity will be to destroy it.

Many of my associates advised me not to write this book because of the person that it will expose and the backlash I may receive as a result of their influence and power. Many said that I may appear to be just another angry Black man trying to fight the system and hating America. Some said that I may appear unpatriotic and radical toward the United States. My reply to them was and is that I will never live in fear of any man. I fear God and God only do I fear. Fear is torment and to live a life of fear is to have a defeated and cowardly existence. Injustice does make me angry but to the contrary I love America that is why I fight and expose it's injustices in an attempt to make the **powers that be** respect and adhere to the constitution of the United States of America. I will always expose the evil and corruption whenever and wherever it can be found and the perpetrators of it.

One of the main purposes for writing this book is to inform prospective attorneys of what the real world of law is all about. Many aspiring attorneys attend law school for numerous reasons and the most noble is to help administer justice to all of America's citizens. Persons desiring to make a career of the legal profession should know that there is more to the law than the theories that they read about in law books. The law is far from an exact science and if you ask twenty judges to rule on the same case you may get twenty different opinions. Many of them bring to the bench their bias and prejudices which sometime supersedes the written law. There is a scripture in the Bible that says get wisdom, knowledge and understanding; but in all of your getting get an understanding for it is the principle thing.

Many names of the person in the stories contained in this book have been changed, but all of the stories are true.

SYSTEMATIC CRONYISM

Let me tell you about my friend Dave and his experience with the court system in Monroe Louisiana

Dan was a hard working young man that grew up in Ouachita Parish. In Louisiana we have one of many dubious distinctions of having parishes instead of counties. Only three states in the Union have divisions other than counties, those being Louisiana, Alaska and New York. Monroe is the county seat for Ouachita Parish.

Dan served in the U.S. Army during part of the Viet Nam era. He grew up in rural West Monroe with his maternal grandparents in the fifties and sixties. Dan did not have a lot of the necessities that most Americans now take for granted. For several years he and his family drank water from a ground spring and for several years from a ground well which went dry. Dental care was not a priority their home. Dan had a lot of dental problems and was advised by a dentist that if he don't get some dental work done that Dan will not have any teeth at age twenty five. The thought of having dentures and those teeth setting in a glass at night frighten him very much. Dan recalled having met this beautiful young lady who apparently had some type of dental disease and had to have all of her teeth extracted. All Dan could visualize was seeing his grandmother's mouth when she would take those teeth out to brush them, and that was the deal breaker. The thought of having no teeth haunted Dan. Where was Dan going to get all of this money to have the dental work done that he need?

One day an army recruiter came to Dan's school and told him about all of the benefits available to soldiers. One of the benefits that caught Dan's attention was the dental benefits. Well that was a good benefit but weighing the option of was against dental benefits didn't seem like a very good deal. But it seems that fate caught up with him and Dan was drafted. Dan decided to make the best of a bad situation so he began his dental treatment in the Army. The dental work was never completed in the Army so Dan was given a voucher to give to a civilian dentist to complete his dental work.

Dan soon found a dentist to do the work but he was not competent at all. He placed a crown in his mouth that covered about three fourths of the tooth. He began to make excuses and told him that this procedure will work fine and if Dan had any problems he would guarantee it for life. Dan, being naive of the dental process went along with the story since he was getting a guarantee. Of course that wasn't true and after short time decay and leaks became a problem. Dan returned to the dentist to have the work corrected using his previous guarantee that the dental would work fine. After he did some patch work Dan informed him of his guarantee and refused to pay him any additional money. After Dan left the dentist office the dentist called his friend at the city prosecutor's office and convinced him to charge Dan with "theft of a dental bill." How one steals a dental bill is still a mystery to me.

Dan knew the assistant city prosecutor in Monroe so Dan decided to talk to him and find out what was this charge was about. After a short visit he assured him that this was simply a lot of "BS" and don't worry about a thing. So Dan followed his advised and didn't worry about a thing. Dan came to court for the arraignment and his charge was read in court. As Dan stood there waiting for the assistant prosecutor to dismiss the charge; he began to go through the process of reading all of the legal documents as was quickly rebuked by Judge Stout. Judge Stout was one of the Monroe's city judges at that time. Judge Stout informed Dan's friend the prosecutor to "just tell that you are charging Mr. Dan with theft of a dental bill." Dan's friend the prosecutor quickly dropped his head and said, "yes you honor" again the judge rebuked him saying, "now that's not what I want to hear; I want you to say that "the city prosecutor office is filing charges of theft of a dental bill against Mr. Dan. " Dan stood there feeling sorry for his friend even though Dan was the one getting the injustice. Dan thought to himself how embarrassing it must be to go through all of those years of education and still be treated like a slave. Dan stood there watching this facade play out in court anxious to see the next move.

The court appointed a lawyer to represent Dan and gave him a trial date. He heard nothing from the attorney until the day of the trial. The dentist was called for cross examination and Dan's so-called attorney crossed examined him with a lot of irrelevant and useless jargon. Dan's attorney asked him about everything except the guarantee that he had promised Dan and the dispute about the money. It soon became apparent to Dan that his attorney had no interest at all in representing him. Dan watched the judge throughout the testimony and the visual messages that was sent to his attorney when he started asking relevant questions. The judge soon ordered a recess, at which time Dan's and his attorney went into a room and he began to whisper to him, "look! the judge said I can get this thing settled, all you have to do is give the dentist a hundred dollars and the judge will just dismiss this case." Dan looked at the court appointed attorney and proceeded to whisper back, "go tell the judge and that other son of a bitch that I ain't giving them a dam thing." The attorney looked at Dan in amazement and said, "ok you are taking a big risk of going to jail." So shortly thereafter the judge found Dan guilty of "theft of a dental bill" and ordered Dan to return in thirty days for sentencing. Dan had always believed that if you hadn't found something in this life worth fighting for then you are probably not fit to live. Dan had never been a coward and refused to let anyone use their powers to abuse him. If he did then he would be endorsing, reinforcing and supporting their illegal and bad behavior. There is a saying, "that if one has not found something worth dying for then he/she is not fit to live." But if one has not found something that he/she is not willing to **KILL** for then they are not fit to live. Dan preferred living for his cause let the wicked die for their cause.

Dan spoke to some of his attorney friends and most agreed that he was in trouble. So Dan did as he always does put it in God's hands and went about his daily activities. About two weeks passed and as usual Dan was watching the local news when this special report came on. They announced that Judge Stout had been sentenced to three years in prison for tax evasion. This was the same judge that was supposed to be sentencing Dan in a couple of weeks.

As fate would have it a few days later Dan was shopping and saw a tall blonde haired guy in the ally in front of him as he approached him he turned to get something off of the shelf and to Dan's surprise it was Judge Stout. Dan spoke to him, "hello Judge I will be praying for you while you're in prison." Well to make a long story short Dan was never sentenced and heard nothing else from the charge until Dan had it expunged.

Unfortunately, too many judges use the bench as a tool to practice cronyism, racism and politics. Unfortunately they can do so with impunity. Everyone involved in this case knew that this was a civil matter to be heard in a civil court and not a criminal one. But all too often in a dispute between a White man and a Black man when the Black man is at the advantage then the matter becomes criminal. Too much of the Louisiana Justice System is based on your lawyer, whether he is court appointed, hired, and whether or not you are represented by one. There are lots of signals being sent from the bench to court appointed lawyer as to whether you get good representation or not. This brings me to the next case in point.

There is a very famous land mark decision case that originated in Jackson Mississippi back in the 1960s' styled Pierson versus Ray (U.S. 547 (1967)). This case arose out of African Americans who attempted to integrate a bus line's waiting room. This was another case of the Blacks in Mississippi saying that, " if I pay the same money then I am entitled to the same services." The petitioners, African American and White preachers traveling together, attempted to use a segregated interstate bus terminal waiting room which displayed a sign saying "Whites Only" in a Jackson, Mississippi bus terminal in 1961s. The preachers upon entering the seating area were told by police that they could not use this area because it was for White people only and they were Negroes. When the preacher insisted upon using the area they were placed under arrest and charged with conduct breaching the peace in violation of a Mississippi Code, which the Supreme Court had already held unconstitutional in *Thomas V. Mississippi, 380 U.S. 524,* as applied to similar facts. Petitioners waived a jury trial, and were convicted by respondent municipal police justice. On appeal, one petitioner was accorded a trial *de novo* and, following a directed verdict in his favor, the cases against the other petitioners were dropped. Petitioners then brought this action in the District Court for damages (1) under 42 U.S.C 1983, which makes liable "every person" who under color of law deprives another person of his civil rights, and (2) at common law for false arrest and imprisonment. The evidence showed that the ministers expected to be arrested upon entering a segregated area. Though the witnesses agreed that petitioners entered the waiting room peacefully, petitioners testified that there was no crowd at the terminal, whereas the police testified that a threatening crowd followed petitioners. The jury found for respondents. On appeal, the Court of Appeals held that (1) respondent police justice had immunity for his judicial acts under both 1983 and the state common law and (2) the policemen had immunity under the state common law of false arrest if they had probable cause to believe 2087.5 valid, since they were not

required to predict what laws are constitutional, but that, by virtue of *Monroe V. Pape,* 365 U.S. 167, they had no such immunity under 1983 where the state statute was subsequently declared invalid. The court remanded the case against the officers for a new trial under 1983 because of prejudicial crossexamination of petitioners, but ruled that they could not recover if it were shown at the new trial that they had gone to Mississippi in anticipation that they would be illegally arrested. This was the court's way of creating a barrier against the petitioners. In the state of Mississippi African American live everyday with the anticipation of being arrested. Any African American who drove a new car in certain Mississippi and other Southern town did so with the anticipation of being arrested. A well- dressed black man did so with the anticipation of being arrested. If he displayed large amounts of cash he could be arrested. The court here is pretending to do justice when in actuality it is trying to give the racist Mississippi police and judge an escape goat, a way out of being liable for their actions
The court held the following in this case:

1. The settled common law principle that a judge is immune from liability for damages for his judicial acts was not abolished by Cf.

Tenney v. Brandhove, 341U.S. 367. Pp. 386 U.S553-555.

2. The defense of good faith and probable cause which is

available to police officers in a common law action for false arrest and imprisonment is available in an action under 1983. Monroe v. Pape. Supra, distinguished, Pp.386U.S. 555-557.

3. Though the officers were not required to predict this Court's ruling in *Thomas v. Mississippi,*

Supra, that 2087.5 was unconstitutional as applied, and the defense of good faith and probable cause is available in an action under $ 1983, it does not follow that the count based thereon shall be dismissed, since the evidence was conflicting as to whether the police had acted in good faith and with probable cause in arresting the petitioners. Pp. 386 U.S. 557-558.

4. Petitioners did not consent to their arrest by deliberately exercising their right to use the waiting room in a peaceful manner with the expectation that they would be illegally arrested P.386 U.S. 558. 352 F. & 213, affirmed in part, reversed in part, and remanded.

4. Petitioners did not consent to their arrest by deliberately exercising their right to use the waiting room in a peaceful manner with the expectation that they would be illegally arrested. P.386 U.S. 558. 352 F. & 213, affirmed in part, reversed in part, and remanded.

MR. CHIEF JUSTICE WARREN delivered the opinion of Court.

These cases present issues involving the liability of local police officers and judges under title 1 of the Civil Rights Act of 1871 Stat. 13, now 42 U.S.C. 1983. Petitioners in No. 79 were members of a group of 15 white and Negro Episcopal clergymen who attempted to use segregated facilities at an interstate bus terminal in Jackson Mississippi, in 1961. They were arrested by respondents Ray, Griffith, and Nichols, policemen of the City of Jackson, and charged with violating 2987.5 of the Mississippi Code, which makes guilty of a misdemeanor anyone who congregates with others in a public place under circumstances such that a breach of the peace may be occasioned thereby, and refuses to move on when ordered to do so by a police officer. Petitioners waived a jury trial and were convicted of the offense the respondent Spencer, a municipal police justice. They were each given the maximum sentence of four months in jail and a fine of $200. On appeal, petitioner Jones was accorded a trial *de novo* in the County Court, and, after the city produced its evidence, the court granted his motion for a directed verdict. The cases against the other petitioners were then dropped.

Having been vindicated in the County Court, petitioners brought this action for damages in the United States District Court for the Southern District of Mississippi, Jackson Division, alleging that respondents had violated 1983, *supra*, and that respondents were liable at common law for false arrest and imprisonment. A jury returned verdicts for respondents on both counts. On appeal, the Court of Appeals for the Fifth Circuit held that respondent Spencer was immune from liability under both 1983 and the common law of Mississippi for acts committed within his judicial jurisdiction. 352F.2d 213. As to the police officers, the court noted that 2087.5 of the Mississippi was held unconstitutional as applied to similar facts in *Thomas v. Mississippi* 380 U.S. 524 (1965). Although *Thomas* was decided years after the arrest involved in this trial, the court held that the policemen would be liable in a suit under 1983 for an unconstitutional arrest even if they acted in good faith and with probable cause in making an arrest under a state statue not yet held invalid. The court believed that this stern result was required by *Monroe v. Pape*.

CERTIORARI TO THE UNITED STATES COURT OF APPEALS

FOR THE FIFTH CIRCUIT

Syllabus

Petitioners, 386 U.S. attempted to use a segregated interstate bus terminal waiting room in Jackson, Mississippi, in 1961. They were arrested by respondent policemen and charged with conduct breaching the peace in violation of § 2087.5 of the Mississippi Code, which this Court, in 1965, held unconstitutional in *Thomas v. Mississippi,* 380 U.S. 524, as applied to similar facts. Petitioners waived a jury trial, and were convicted by respondent municipal police justice. On appeal, one petitioner was accorded a trial *de novo* and, following a directed verdict in his favor, the cases against the other petitioners were dropped. Petitioners then brought this action in the District Court for damages (1) under 42 U.S.C. § 1983, which makes liable "every person" who under color of law deprives another person of his civil rights, and (2) at common law for false arrest and imprisonment. The evidence showed that the ministers expected to be arrested on entering a segregated area. Though the witnesses agreed that petitioners entered the waiting room peacefully, petitioners testified that there was no crowd at the terminal, whereas the police testified that a threatening crowd followed petitioners. The jury found for respondents. On appeal, the Court of Appeals held that (1) respondent police justice had immunity for his judicial acts under both § 1983 and the state common law and (2) the policemen had immunity under the state common law of false arrest if they had probable cause to believe § 2087.5 valid, since they were not required to predict what laws are constitutional, but that, by virtue of *Monroe v. Pape,* 365 U.S. 167, they had no such immunity under § 1983 where the state statute was subsequently declared invalid. The court remanded the case against the officers for a new trial under § 1983 because of prejudicial cross-examination of petitioners, but ruled that they could not recover if it were shown at the new trial that they had gone to Mississippi in anticipation that they would be illegally arrested. This is one of the most foolish things that I have ever heard coming out of the mouth of a judge. In other words if a Black person thought that he would get arrested for walking the street, he should just stay at home for the rest of his life.

Held:

1. The settled common law principle that a judge is immune from liability for damages for his judicial acts was not abolished by § 1983. *Cf. Tenney v. Brandhove,* 341 U.S. 367. Pp. 386 U.S. 553555,

2. The defense of good faith and probable cause which is available to police officers in a common law action for false arrest and imprisonment is also available in an action under § 1983. *Monroe v. Pape, supra,* distinguished. Pp. 386 U.S. 555-557.

3. Though the officers were not required to predict this Court's ruling in *Thomas v. Mississippi, supra,* that § 2087.5 was unconstitutional as applied, and the defense of good faith and probable cause is available in an action under § 1983, it does not follow that the count based thereon should be dismissed, since the evidence was conflicting as to whether the police had acted

in good faith and with probable cause in arresting the petitioners. Pp. 386 U.S .558

4. Petitioners did not consent to their arrest by deliberately exercising their right to use the waiting room in a peaceful manner with the expectation that they would be illegally arrested. P. 386 U.S. 358, 352 F. & 213, affirmed in part, reversed in part, and remanded.

MR. CHIEF JUSTICE WARREN delivered the opinion of Court.

These cases present issues involving the liability of local police officers and judges under § 1 of the Civil Rights Act of 1871, 17 Stat. 13, now 42 U.S.C. § 1983. Petitioner in No. 79 were members of a group of 15 white and Negro Episcopal clergymen who attempted to use segregated facilities at an interstate bus terminal in Jackson Mississippi, in 1961. They were arrested by respondents Ray, Griffith, and Nichols, policemen of the City of Jackson, and charged with violating § 2087.5 of the Mississippi Code, which makes guilty of a misdemeanor anyone who congregates with others in a public place under circumstances such that a breach of the peace may be occasioned thereby, and refuses to move on when ordered to do so by a police officer. Petitioners waived a jury trial and were convicted of the offense by respondent Spencer, a municipal police justice. They were each given the maximum sentence of four months in jail and a fine of $200. On appeal, petitioner Jones was accorded a trial *de novo* in the County Court, and, after the city produced its evidence, the court granted his motion for a directed verdict. The cases against the other petitioners were then dropped.

Having been vindicated in the County Court, petitioners brought this action for damages in the United States District Court for the Southern District of Mississippi, Jackson Division, alleging that respondents had violated § 1983, *supra,* and that respondents were liable at common law for false arrest and imprisonment. A jury returned verdicts for respondents on both counts. On appeal, the Court of Appeals for the Fifth Circuit held that respondent Spencer was immune from liability under both § 1983 and the common law of Mississippi for acts committed within his judicial jurisdiction. 352 F.2d 213. As to the police officers, the court noted that § 2087.5 of the Mississippi Code was held unconstitutional as applied to similar facts in *Thomas v. Mississippi,380 U.S. 524* (1965) Although *Thomas* was decided years after the arrest involved in this trial, the court held that the policemen would be liable in a suit under § 1983 for an unconstitutional arrest even if they acted in good faith and with probable cause in making an arrest under a state statute not yet held invalid. The court believed that this stern result was required by Monroe v. Pape, 365 U.S. (1961). Under the count based on the common law of Mississippi, however, it held that the policemen would not be liable if they had probable cause to believe that the statute had been violated, because Mississippi law does not require police officers to predict at their peril which state laws are constitutional and which are not. Apparently dismissing the common law claim, the Court of Appeals reversed and remanded for a new trial on the § 1983 claim against the police officers because defense counsel had been allowed to cross-examine the ministers on various irrelevant and prejudicial matters, particularly including an alleged convergence of their views on racial justice with those of the Communist Party. At the new trial, however, the court held that the ministers could not recover if it were proved that they went to Mississippi anticipating that they would be illegally arrested, because such action would constitute consent to the arrest under the principle of *volenti non fit injuria,* he who consents to a wrong cannot be injured.

We granted certiorari in No. 79 to consider whether a local judge is liable for damages under § 1983 for an unconstitutional conviction and whether the ministers should be denied recovery against the police officers if they acted with the anticipation that they would be illegally arrested. We also granted the police officers' petition in No. 94 to determine if the Court of Appeals correctly held that they could not assert the defense of good faith and probable cause to an action under § 1983 for unconstitutional arrest. Notice the words used by the judges such volenti non fit injuria and certiorari Latin words used to intimidate and confuse persons who are not lawyers.

The evidence at the federal trial showed that petitioners and other Negro and white Episcopal clergymen undertook a "prayer pilgrimage" in 1961 from New Orleans to Detroit. The purpose of the pilgrimage was to visit church institutions and other places in the North and South to promote racial equality and integration, and, finally, to report to a church convention in Detroit. Letters from the leader of the group to its members indicate that the clergymen intended from the beginning to go to Jackson and attempt to use segregated facilities at the bus terminal there, and that they fully expected to be arrested for doing so. The group made plans based on the assumption that they would be arrested if they attempted peacefully to exercise their right as interstate travelers to use the waiting rooms and other facilities at the bus terminal, and the letters discussed arrangements for bail and other matters relevant to arrests.

The ministers stayed one night in Jackson, and went to the bus terminal the next morning to depart for Chattanooga, Tennessee. They entered the waiting room, disobeying a sign at the entrance that announced "White Waiting Room Only" By

Order of the Police Department." They then turned to enter the small terminal restaurant, but were stopped by two Jackson police officers, respondents Griffith and Nichols, who had been awaiting their arrival and who ordered them to "move on." The ministers replied that they wanted to eat, and refused to move on. Respondent Ray, then a police captain and now the deputy chief of police, arrived a few minutes later. The ministers were placed under arrest and taken to the jail.

All witnesses, including the police officers, agreed that the ministers entered the waiting room peacefully and engaged in no boisterous or objectionable conduct while in the "White Only" area. There was conflicting testimony on the number of bystanders present and their behavior. Petitioners testified that there was no crowd at the station that no one followed them into the waiting room, and that no one uttered threatening words or made threatening gestures. The police testified that some 25 to 30 persons followed the ministers into the terminal, that persons in the crowd were in a very dissatisfied and ugly mood, and that they were mumbling and making unspecified threatening gestures. The police did not describe any specific threatening incidents, and testified that they took no action against any persons in the crowd who were threatening violence because they "had determined that the ministers was the cause of the violence if any might occur," although the ministers were respectful, orderly and polite and the police did not claim that it was beyond their power to control the allegedly disorderly crowd. The arrests and convictions were followed by this lawsuit.

We find no difficulty in agreeing with the Court of Appeals that Judge Spencer is immune from liability for damages for his role in these convictions. The record is barren of any proof or specific allegation that Judge Spencer played any role in these arrests and convictions other than to adjudge petitioners guilty when their cases came before his court. Few doctrines were more solidly established at common law than the immunity of judges from liability for damages for acts committed within their judicial jurisdiction, as this Court recognized when it adopted the doctrine in Bradley v. Fisher, 13 Wall. 335 (1872). This immunity applies even when the judge is accused of acting maliciously and corruptly, and it "is not for the protection or benefit of a malicious or corrupt judge, but for the benefit of the public, whose interest it is that the judges should be at liberty to exercise their functions with independence and without fear of consequences."

(*Scott v. Stansfield,* L.R. 3 Ex. 220, 223 (1868), quoted in *Bradley v. Fisher, supra,* 80 U.S. 349, note, at 80 U.S.350.) It is a judge's duty to decide all cases within his jurisdiction that are brought before him, including controversial cases that arouse the most intense feelings in the litigants. His errors may be corrected on appeal, but he should not have to fear that unsatisfied litigants may hound him with litigation charging malice or corruption. Imposing such a burden on judges would contribute not to principled and fearless decision making, but to intimidation.

We do not believe that this settled principle of law was abolished by § 1983, which makes liable "every person" who under color of law deprives another person of his civil rights. The legislative record gives no clear indication that Congress meant to abolish wholesale all common law immunities. Accordingly, this Court held in *Tenney v. Brandhove,* 341 U.S.361 (1951), that the immunity of legislators for acts within the legislative role was not abolished. The immunity of judges for acts within the judicial role is equally well established, and we presume that Congress would have specifically so provided had it wished to abolish the doctrine.

The common law has never granted police officers an absolute and unqualified immunity, and the officers in this case do not claim that they are entitled to one. Their claim is, rather, that they should not be liable if they acted in good faith and with probable cause in making an arrest under a statute that they believed to be valid. Under the prevailing view in this country, a peace officer who arrests someone with probable cause is not liable for false arrest simply because the innocence of the suspect is later proved. Restatement, Second, Torts § 121 (1965); 1 Harper & James, The Law of Torts § 3.18, at 277-278 (1956); *Ward v. Fidelity & Deposit Co. of Maryland,* 179 F.2d 327 (C.A. 8th Cir.1950). A policeman's lot is not so unhappy that he must choose between being charged with dereliction of duty if he does not arrest when he has probable cause and being mulcted in damages if he does. Although the matter is not entirely free from doubt, the same consideration would seem to require excusing him from liability for acting under a statute that he reasonably believed to be valid, but that was later held unconstitutional, on its face or as applied.

The Court of Appeals held that the officers had such a limited privilege under the common law of Mississippi, and indicated that it would have recognized a similar privilege under § 1983 except that it felt compelled to hold otherwise by our decision in Monroe v. Pape, 365 U.S. 167 (1961). *Monroe v. Pape* presented no question of immunity, however, and none was decided. The complaint in that case alleged that "13 Chicago police officers broke into petitioners' home in the early morning, routed them from bed, made them stand naked in the living room, and ransacked every room, emptying drawers and ripping mattress covers. It further alleged that Mr. Monroe was then taken to the police station and detained on 'open' charges for 10 hours while he was interrogated about a two-day-old murder, that he was not taken before a magistrate, though one was accessible, that he was not permitted to call his family or attorney, that he was subsequently released without criminal charges' being preferred against him." 365 U.S. at 365 U.S. 169. The police officers did not choose to go to trial and defend the case on the hope that they could convince a jury that they believed in good faith that it was their duty to assault Monroe and his family in this manner. Instead, they sought dismissal of the complaint, contending principally that their activities were so plainly illegal under state law that they did not act "under color of any statute, ordinance, regulation, custom, or usage, of any State or Territory," as required by § 1983. In rejecting this argument, we in no way intimated that the defense of good faith and probable cause was foreclosed by the statute. We also held that the complaint should not be dismissed for failure to state that the officers had "a specific intent to deprive a person of a federal right," but this holding, which related to requirements of pleading, carried no implications as to which defenses would be available to the police officers. As we went on to say in the same paragraph, § 1983 "should be read against the background of tort liability that makes a man responsible for the natural consequences of his actions." 365 U.S. at 365 U.S. 187. Part of the background of tort liability, in the case of police officers making an arrest, is the defense of good faith and probable cause.

We hold that the defense of good faith and probable cause, which the Court of Appeals found available to the officers in the common law action for false arrest and imprisonment, is also available to them in the action under § 1983. This holding does not, however, mean that the count based thereon should be dismissed. The Court of Appeals ordered dismissal of the common law count on the theory that the police officers were not required to predict our decision in *Thomas v. Mississippi,* 380 U.S. 524. We agree that a police officer is not charged with predicting the future course of constitutional law. But the petitioners in this case did not simply argue that they were arrested under a statute later held unconstitutional. They claimed and attempted to prove that the police officers arrested them solely for attempting to use the "White Only" waiting room, that no crowd was present, and that no one threatened violence or seemed about to cause a disturbance. The officers did not defend on the theory that they believed in good faith that it was constitutional to arrest the ministers solely for using the waiting room. Rather, they claimed and attempted to prove that they did not arrest the ministers for the purpose of preserving the custom of segregation in Mississippi, but solely for the purpose of preventing violence.

They testified, in contradiction to the ministers, that a crowd gathered and that imminent violence was likely. If the jury believed the testimony of the officers and disbelieved that of the ministers, and if the jury found that the officers reasonably believed in good faith that the arrest was constitutional, then a verdict for the officers would follow even though the arrest was, in fact, unconstitutional. The jury did resolve the factual issues in favor of the officers but, for reasons previously stated, its verdict was influenced by irrelevant and prejudicial evidence. Accordingly, the case must be remanded to the trial court for a new trial.

It is necessary to decide what importance should be given at the new trial to the substantially undisputed fact that the petitioners went to Jackson expecting to be illegally arrested. We do not agree with the Court of Appeals that they somehow consented to the arrest because of their anticipation that they would be illegally arrested, even assuming that they went to the Jackson bus terminal for the sole purpose of testing their rights to unsegregated public accommodations. The case contains no proof or allegation that they in any way tricked or goaded the officers into arresting them. The petitioners had the right to use the waiting room of the Jackson bus terminal, and their deliberate exercise of that right in a peaceful, orderly, and inoffensive manner, does not disqualify them from seeking damages under § 1983.

The judgment of the Court of Appeals is affirmed in part and reversed in part, and the cases are remanded for further proceedings consistent with this opinion.

It is so ordered.

* Together with No. 94, *Ray et al. v. Pierson et al.,* also on certiorari to the same court.

"Every person who, under color of any statute, ordinance, regulation, custom, or usage, of any State or Territory, subjects, or causes to be subjected, any citizen of the United States or other person within the jurisdiction thereof to the deprivation of any rights, privileges, or immunities secured by the Constitution and laws, shall be liable to the party injured in an action at law, suit in equity, or other proper proceeding for redress."

42 U.S.C. § 1983.

["1. Whoever with intent to provoke a breach of the peace, or under circumstances such that a breach of the peace may he occasioned thereby:"

"(1) crowds or congregates with others in . . . any hotel, motel, store, restaurant, lunch counter, cafeteria, sandwich shop, . . . or any other place of business engaged in selling or serving members of the public, or in or around any free entrance to any such place of business or public building, or to any building owned by another individual, or a corporation, or a partnership or an association, and who fails or refuses to disperse and move on, or disperse or move on, when ordered so to do by any law enforcement officer of any municipality, or county, in which such act or acts are committed, or by any law enforcement officer of the State of Mississippi, or any other authorized person, . . . shall be guilty of disorderly conduct, which is made a misdemeanor, and, upon conviction thereof, shall be punished by a fine of not more than two hundred dollars ($200.00), or imprisonment in the county jail for not more than four (4) months, or by both such fine and imprisonment. . . ." The ministers involved in No. 79 will be designated as "petitioners" throughout this opinion, although they are the respondents in No. 94.

In *Thomas,* various "Freedom Riders" were arrested and convicted under circumstances substantially similar to the facts of these cases. The police testified that they ordered the "Freedom Riders" to leave because they feared that onlookers might breach the peace. We reversed without argument or opinion, citing *Boynton v. Virginia,* 364 U.S. 454 (1960). *Boynton* held that racial discrimination in a bus terminal restaurant utilized as an integral part of the transportation of interstate passengers violates § 216(d) of the Interstate Commerce Act. State enforcement of such discrimination is barred by the Supremacy Clause.

Respondents read the court's opinion as remanding for a new trial on this claim. The court stated, however, that the officers "are immune from liability for false imprisonment at common law, but not from liability for violations of the Federal statutes on civil rights. It therefore follows that there should be a new trial of the civil rights claim against the appellee police officers so that there may be a determination of the fact issue as to whether the appellants invited or consented to the arrest and imprisonment."

Respondents did not challenge in their petition in No. 94 the holding of the Court of Appeals that a new trial is necessary because of the prejudicial cross-examination. Belatedly, they devoted a section of their brief to the contention that the crossexamination was proper. This argument is no more meritorious than it is timely. The views of the Communist Party on racial equality were not an issue in these cases.

Transcript of Record, at 347. (Testimony of Officer Griffith.) Petitioners attempted to suggest a "conspiracy" between Judge Spencer and the police officers by questioning him about his reasons for finding petitioners guilty in these cases and by showing that he had found other "Freedom Riders" guilty under similar circumstances in previous cases. The proof of conspiracy never went beyond this suggestion that inferences could be drawn from Judge Spencer's judicial decisions. *See* Transcript of Record at 35-371.

Since our decision in *Tenney v. Brandhove, supra,* the courts of appeals have consistently held that judicial immunity is a defense to an action under § 1983. *See Bauers v. Heisel,* 361 F.2d 581 (C.A.3d Cir.1966), and cases cited therein.

See Caveat, Restatement, Second, Torts § 121, at 207-208 (1965); *Miller v. Stinnett,* 257 F.2d 910 (C.A. 10th Cir.1958).

See Golden v. Thompson, 194 Miss. 241, 11 So.2d 906 (1943).

The petition for certiorari in No. 79 also presented the question whether the Court of Appeals correctly dismissed the count based on the common law of Mississippi. We do not ordinarily review the holding of a court of appeals on a matter of state law, and we find no reason for departing from that tradition in this case. The state common law claim in this case is merely cumulative, and petitioners' right to recover for an invasion of their civil rights, subject to the defense of good faith and probable cause, is adequately secured by § 1983.

MR. JUSTICE DOUGLAS, dissenting.

I do not think that all judges, under all circumstances, no matter how outrageous their conduct, are immune (Page 386 U. S. 559) from suit under 17 Stat. 13, 42 U.S.C. § 1983. The Court's ruling is not justified by the admitted need for a vigorous and independent judiciary, is not commanded by the common law doctrine of judicial immunity, and does not follow inexorably from our prior decisions.

The statute, which came on the books as § 1 of the Ku Klux Klan Act of April 20, 1871, 17 Stat. 13, provides that "every person" who, under color of state law or custom, "subjects, or causes to be subjected, any citizen . . . to the deprivation of any rights, privileges, or immunities secured by the Constitution and laws, shall be liable to the party injured in an action at law, suit in equity, or other proper proceeding for redress."

To most, "every person" would mean every person, not every person except judges. Despite the plain import of those words, the Court decided in *Tenney v. Brandhove,* 341 U.S. 367, that state legislators are immune from suit as long as the deprivation of civil rights which they caused a person occurred while the legislators "were acting in a field where legislators traditionally have power to act." *Id.* at 341 U.S. 379. I dissented from the creation of that judicial exception, as I do from the creation of the present one.

The congressional purpose seems to me to be clear. A condition of lawlessness existed in certain of the States under which people were being denied their civil rights. Congress intended to provide a remedy for the wrongs being perpetrated. And its members were not unaware that certain members of the judiciary were implicated in the state of affairs which the statute was intended to rectify. It was often noted that "immunity is given to crime, and the records of the public tribunals are searched in vain for any evidence of effective redress." Cong.Globe, 42d Cong., 1st Sess., 374. Mr. Rainey of South Carolina noted that "The courts are in many instances under the control of those who are wholly inimical to the impartial administration of law and equity." *Id.* at 394. (Page 386 U. S. 560)

Congressman Beatty of Ohio claimed that it was the duty of Congress to listen to the appeals of those who, "by reason of popular sentiment or secret organizations or prejudiced juries or bribed judges, [cannot] obtain the rights and privileges due an American citizen. . . ."

Id. at 429. The members supporting the proposed measure were apprehensive that there had been a complete breakdown in the administration of justice in certain States, and that laws nondiscriminatory on their face were being applied in a discriminatory manner, that the newly won civil rights of the Negro were being ignored, and that the Constitution was being defied. It was against this background that the section was passed, and it is against this background that it should be interpreted.

It is said that, at the time of the statute's enactment, the doctrine of judicial immunity was well settled, and that Congress cannot be presumed to have intended to abrogate the doctrine, since it did not clearly evince such a purpose. This view is beset by many difficulties. It assumes that Congress could and should specify in advance all the possible circumstances to which a remedial statute might apply and state which cases are within the scope of a statute.

"Underlying [this] view is an atomistic conception of intention, coupled with what may be called a pointer theory of meaning. This view conceives the mind to be directed toward individual things, rather than toward general ideas, toward distinct situations of fact, rather than toward some significance in human affairs that these situations may share. If this view were taken seriously, then we would have to regard the intention of the draftsman of a statute directed against 'dangerous weapons' as being directed toward an endless series of individual objects: revolvers, (Page 386 U. S. 561) automatic pistols, daggers, Bowie knives, etc. If a court applies the statute to a weapon its draftsman had not thought of, then it would be 'legislating,' not 'interpreting,' as even more obviously it would be if it were to apply the statute to a weapon not yet invented when the statute was passed." (Fuller, The Morality of Law 84 (1964).

Congress, of course, acts in the context of existing common law rules, and, in construing a statute, a court considers the "common law before the making of the Act." *Heydon's Case,* 3 Co.Rep. 7a, 76 Eng.Rep. 637 (Ex. 1584). But Congress enacts a statute to remedy the inadequacies of the preexisting law, including the common law. It cannot be presumed that the common law is the perfection of reason, is superior to statutory law (Sedgwick, Construction of Statutes 270 (1st ed. 1857); Pound, Common Law and Legislation, 21 Harv.L.Rev. 383, 404406 (1908)), and that the legislature always changes law for the worse. Nor should the canon of construction "statutes in derogation of the common law are to be strictly construed" be applied so as to weaken a remedial statute whose purpose is to remedy the defects of the preexisting law.

The position that Congress did not intend to change the common law rule of judicial immunity ignores the fact that every member of Congress who spoke to the issue assumed that the words of the statute meant what they said, and that judges would be liable. Many members of Congress objected to the statute because it imposed (Page 386 U. S. 562) liability on members of the judiciary. Mr. Arthur of Kentucky opposed the measure because: "Hitherto . . . no judge or court has been held liable, civilly or criminally, for judicial acts. . . . Under the provisions of [section 1], every judge in the State court . . . will enter upon and pursue the call of official duty with the sword of Damocles suspended over him. . . ."

Cong.Globe, 42d Cong., 1st Sess., 365-366. And Senator Thurman noted that:

"There have been two or three instances already under the civil rights bill of State judges being taken into the United States district court, sometimes upon indictment for the offense . . . of honestly and conscientiously deciding the law to be as they understood it to be. . . ."

"Is [section 1] intended to perpetuate that? Is it intended to enlarge it? Is it intended to extend it so that no longer a judge sitting on the bench to decide causes can decide them free from any fear except that of impeachment, which never lies in the absence of corrupt motive? Is that to be extended so that every judge of a State may be liable to be dragged before some Federal judge to vindicate his opinion and to be mulcted in damages if that Federal judge shall think the opinion was erroneous? That is the language of this bill."

Cong.Globe, 42d Cong., 1st Sess., Appendix 217. Mr. Lewis of Kentucky expressed the fear that:

"By the first section, in certain cases, the judge of a State court, though acting under oath of office, is made liable to a suit in the Federal court and subject to damages for his decision against a suitor. . . ."

Cong.Globe, 42d Cong., 1st Sess., 385.

Page 386 U. S. 563

Yet, despite the repeated fears of its opponents and the explicit recognition that the section would subject judges to suit, the section remained as it was proposed: it applied to "any person." There was no exception for members of the judiciary. In light of the sharply contested nature of the issue of judicial immunity, it would be reasonable to assume that the judiciary would have been expressly exempted from the wide sweep of the section if Congress had intended such a result.

The section's purpose was to provide redress for the deprivation of civil rights. It was recognized that certain members of the judiciary were instruments of oppression, and were partially responsible for the wrongs to be remedied. The parade of cases coming to this Court shows that a similar condition now obtains in some of the States. Some state courts have been instruments of suppression of civil rights. The methods may have changed; the means may have become more subtle; but the wrong to be remedied still exists.

Today's decision is not dictated by our prior decisions. In *Ex parte Virginia, 100 U.S. 339*, the Court held that a judge who excluded Negroes from juries could be held liable under the Act of March 1, 1875 (18 Stat. 335), one of the Civil Rights Acts. The Court assumed that the judge was merely performing a ministerial function. But it went on to state that the judge would be liable under the statute even if his actions were judicial. It is one thing to say that the common law doctrine of (Page 386 U. S. 564) judicial immunity is a defense to a common law cause of action. But it is quite another to say that the common law immunity rule is a defense to liability which Congress has imposed upon "any officer or other person," as in *Ex parte Virginia,* or upon "every person," as in these cases.

The immunity which the Court today grants the judiciary is not necessary to preserve an independent judiciary. If the threat of civil action lies in the background of litigation, so the argument goes, judges will be reluctant to exercise the discretion and judgment inherent in their position and vital to the effective operation of the judiciary. We should, of course, not protect a member of the judiciary "who is, in fact, guilty of using his powers to vent his spleen upon others, or for any other personal motive not connected with the public good." *Gregoire v. Biddle,* 177 F.2d 579, 581. To deny recovery to a person injured by the ruling of a judge acting for personal gain or out of personal motives would be "monstrous." *Ibid.* But it is argued that absolute immunity is necessary to prevent the chilling effects of a judicial inquiry, or the threat of such inquiry, into whether, in fact, a judge has been unfaithful to his oath of office. Thus, it is necessary to protect the guilty as well as the innocent. The doctrine of separation of powers is, of course, applicable only to the relations of coordinate branches of the same government, not to the relations between the (Page 386 U. S. 565) branches of the Federal Government and those of the States. *See Baker v. Carr,* 369 U.S. 186, 369 U.S. 186. Any argument that Congress could not impose liability on state judges for the deprivation of civil rights would thus have to be based upon the claim that doing so would violate the theory of division of powers between the Federal and State Governments. This claim has been foreclosed by the cases recognizing "that Congress has the power to enforce provisions of the Fourteenth Amendment against those who carry a badge of authority of a State. . . ." *Monroe v. Pape,* 365 U.S. 167, 365 U.S 167-172. In terms of the power of Congress, I can see no difference between imposing liability on a state police officer (*Monroe v. Pape, supra*) and on a state judge. The question presented is not of constitutional dimension; it is solely a question of statutory interpretation.

The argument that the actions of public officials must not be subjected to judicial scrutiny because to do so would have an inhibiting effect on their work is but a more sophisticated manner of saying "The King can do no wrong." Chief Justice Cockburn long ago disposed of the argument that liability would deter judges:

"I cannot believe that judges . . . would fail to discharge their duty faithfully and fearlessly according to their oaths and consciences . . . from any fear of exposing themselves to actions at law. I am persuaded that the number of such actions would be infinitely small, and would be easily disposed of. (Page 386 U. S. 566)

While, on the other hand, I can easily conceive cases in which judicial opportunity might be so perverted and abused for the purpose of injustice as that, on sound principles, the authors of such wrong ought to be responsible to the parties wronged."

Dawkins v. Lord Paulet, L.R. 5 Q.B. 94, 110 (C.J. Cockburn, dissenting).

This is not to say that a judge who makes an honest mistake should be subjected to civil liability. It is necessary to exempt judges from liability for the consequences of their honest mistakes. The judicial function involves an informed exercise of judgment. It is often necessary to choose between differing versions of fact, to reconcile opposing interests, and to decide closely contested issues. Decisions must often be made in the heat of trial. A vigorous and independent mind is needed to perform such delicate tasks. It would be unfair to require a judge to exercise his independent judgment and then to punish him for having exercised it in a manner which, in retrospect, was erroneous. Imposing liability for mistaken, though honest judicial acts, would curb the independent mind and spirit needed to perform judicial functions. Thus, a judge who sustains a conviction on what he forthrightly considers adequate evidence should not be subjected to liability when an appellate court decides that the evidence was not adequate. Nor should a judge who allows a conviction under what is later held an unconstitutional statute.

But that is far different from saying that a judge shall be immune from the consequences of any of his judicial actions, and that he shall not be liable for the knowing and intentional deprivation of a person's civil rights. What about the judge who conspires with local law enforcement officers to "railroad" a dissenter? What about the judge who knowingly turns a trial into a "kangaroo" court? Or one who intentionally flouts the (Page 386 U. S. 567) Constitution in order to obtain a conviction? Congress, I think, concluded that the evils of allowing intentional, knowing deprivations of civil rights to go unredressed far outweighed the speculative inhibiting effects which might attend an inquiry into a judicial deprivation of civil rights. The plight of the oppressed is indeed serious. Under *City of Greenwood v. Peacock,* 384 U.S. 808, the defendant cannot remove to a federal court to prevent a state court from depriving him of his civil rights. And under the rule announced today, the person cannot recover damages for the deprivation.

"Remedial statutes are to be liberally construed." *See generally* Llewellyn, Remarks on the Theory of Appellate Decision and the Rules or Canons About How Statutes Are To Be Construed, 3 Vand.L.Rev. 395 (1950); Llewellyn, The Common

Law Tradition, Appendix C (1960). As altered by the reviser who prepared the Revised Statutes of 1878, and as printed in 42 U.S.C. § 1983, the statute refers to "every person," rather than to "any person."

The opinion in *Ex parte Virginia, supra,* did not mention Bradley v. Fisher, 13 Wall. 335, which held that a judge could not be held liable for causing the name of an attorney to be struck from the court rolls. But in *Bradley,* the action was not brought under any of the Civil Rights Acts.

Other justifications for the doctrine of absolute immunity have been advanced: (1) preventing threat of suit from influencing decision; (2) protecting judges from liability for honest mistakes; (3) relieving judges of the time and expense of defending suits; (4) removing an impediment to responsible men entering the judiciary; (5) necessity of finality; (6) appellate review is satisfactory remedy; (7) the judge's duty is to the public and not to the individual; (8) judicial self-protection; (9) separation of powers. *See generally* Jennings, Tort Liability of Administrative Officers, 21 Minn.L.Rev. 263, 271-272 (1937).

Historically, judicial immunity was a corollary to that theory. Since the King could do no wrong, the judges, his delegates for dispensing justice, "ought not to be drawn into question for any supposed corruption [for this tends] to the slander of the justice of the King." *Floyd & Barker,* 12 Co.Rep. 23, 25, 77 Eng.Rep. 1305, 1307 (Star Chamber 1607). Because the judges were the personal delegates of the King, they should be answerable to him alone. @ 74U.S. 539.

A judge is liable for injury caused by a ministerial act; to have immunity, the judge must be performing a judicial function. *See, e.g., 100 U.S. 100U.S.33*; 2 Harper & James, The Law of Torts, 1642-1643 (1956). The presence of malice and the intention to deprive a person of his constitutional rights he exercises no discretion or individual judgment; he acts no longer as a judge, but as a "minister" of his own prejudices.

THE GREAT DECIEVERS

As one can see many the judges were simply looking for excuses to practice their racisms and prejudices with impunity. It doesn't take a rocket scientist to know that judges do not need immunity against law suits. If a judge is sued he automatically goes before another judge a peer. If his peers find the suit to be frivolous, it is thrown out most often at the plaintiff expense. In addition to having unfair suits against judges thrown out the court can always place sanctions (fines) upon the petitioner. For judges to say that they need immunity is simple a facade and a cloak to hide behind while carrying out their personal prejudices, illegal and corrupt actions. The mere fact that the plaintiff will be held liable for the court cost will deter the filing of frivolous suits in addition to the intimidation factor of filing a suit against an innocent judge. As you probably know that no judge is going to rule against another judge unless there is solid evidence of wrong doing.

The most ludicrous of all the statements made by the so-called justices was the statement that if these people enter the waiting room or restaurant with the knowledge or anticipation of being arrested then the arrest and imprisonment should be upheld. In Mississippi a Black man could get arrested for looking at a White woman. Under these judges theory every time a Black man came across the path of a White Woman he should close his eyes to avoid the possibility of being arrested. In Mendenhall Mississippi Black men until the late 1960's were not allowed to talk loud or the town marshal would simply walk up to them and hit them over the head with his night stick. A good friend and renowned civil rights activist Rev. Spencer Perkins brother was shot down in cold blooded murder by the city marshal because he was talking loud with a group of Black men after sun down which the city marshal did not allow.

Established at common law than the immunity of judges from liability for damages for acts committed within their judicial jurisdiction, as this Court recognized when it adopted the doctrine in Bradley v. Fisher, 13 Wall. 335 (1872). This immunity applies even when the judge is accused of acting maliciously and corruptly.

The rule by the Supreme Court Judges states, "is not for the protection or benefit of a malicious or corrupt judge, but for the benefit of the public, whose interest it is that the judges should be at liberty to exercise their functions with independence and without fear of consequences." In actuality their rule did exactly what they stated it was not intended to do promote malicious and corrupt judges.

We find no difficulty in agreeing with the Court of Appeals that Judge Spencer is immune from liability for damages for his role in these convictions. The record is barren of any proof or specific allegation that Judge Spencer played any role in these arrests and convictions other than to adjudge petitioners guilty when their cases came before his court. Few doctrines were more solidly. Premptive challenges are a favorite tool of used by many racist to fix the jury in such a manner that it eliminates most Blacks and minorities from juries. Each lawyer in Louisiana has up to twelve premptive challenges. this means he can eliminated a prospective juror for any reason. This injustice could be eliminated by attorney having only three premptive challenges.

JUDICIAL TERRORIST

Many of the judges in the above case actually wanted was to place themselves above the law. By placing themselves above the law it would give them carte blanc to harass, terrorize and intimidate persons who were not of the status quo or do favor for kickbacks and under the table money. I have experienced a lot of this in the Nineteenth Judicial District Court.

Many of the problems Americans face abroad is a result of the disrespectful manner in which they have treated socalled "third world countries." What many people don't realize is that the seeds you plant in this life will be the harvest you reap. If you plant seeds of violence and disrespect that is what you will reap. A prime example of this is Robert Kennedy who served as Attorney General to the United States. During the administration of president Johnson there was an uprising throughout this country of African Americans who wanted their civil rights. Many brave Whites and African American banded together and became what is known as "freed riders." They got on buses and rode throughout the south for the purpose of desegregating of public facilities. They also went to Washington D.C. to the democratic national committee to be appointed as delegates. This troubled President Lyndon Johnson because he didn't want to become aligned with African American.

He believed if he became too close to the civil rights struggle that it would hurt his re-election campaign with southern racist.

President Johnson and Robert Kennedy conspired together to derail the civil rights struggle. They conspired with the governor of Mississippi to allow him to jail the freedom riders and civil rights activist in an attempt to sabotage the movement. They jailed and terrorize hundreds of peoples in small inhuman conditions without due process of law or any consideration for the law.

Robert Kennedy and Lyndon Johnson planted seeds of injustice, violence and corruption. The irony is that the seeds of violence Robert Kennedy planted came back to haunt him as he was killed by an assassin's bullet.

Extortion of Children

I have seen so many instances where children are taken out of the home by the Office of Children Services because they were spanked and got a scratch on the hand. When I was a child that would be a cause of celebration if all I got from a spanking was a scratch. The parents are often put through hell and unnecessary legal loops because some social worker doesn't believe in spanking. Often the child is put in a foster home where his behavior becomes exponentially worse, but the state does not have to be accountable for it's irresponsible actions. Only the parents are held responsible for the child's behavior. The parents are often made to pay child support when the child is removed from home and placed in foster care. But before the child gets a penny the District Attorney's office takes money that should be going to the child; of course they call it some kind of fee that is supposed to legitimize it. Citizens of the state of Louisiana pay huge taxes to run these offices. There is no need to take money that is supposed to go to care for children.

It's amazing what some people and organizations will do for money. One of the biggest tricks that I have found that the justice system uses to extort people out of their money with impunity is to give the extortion a pretty name. One of such programs the former District Attorney of East Baton Rouge, Parish operates called the juvenile diversion program.

I was busy at my desk working on a Monday morning about 11:00 a.m. when the telephone rang. No other personnel was available so I answered it with the usual greeting of "hello CRS may I help you." I had no idea that this call would be a call that would bring about a transformation in my life as well as I hope to others that read this book.

This experience has epitomized my belief that nothing happens by accident. All experiences serve some purpose in the recipient's life. The telephone call will serve as the conduits by which this book was written. Had I not received this call and learn of the unjust and criminal acts being levied against Black and poor children I would probably never would have written this book.

On the other end of the telephone was a frantic African American mother looking for help for her daughter. From the information the mother gave me her daughter had some legal problems. From the background information the mother gave me the daughter seemed to be a normal twelve year old girl who did well in school and had no other discipline problems except for getting into a fight at school. The mother stated that her daughter, who for privacy purpose I will call Sara; had never been involved in any discipline problems nor fights at school or any other place. A follow-up investigation into the incident and the child's background revealed this to be accurate.

Sara was very pretty and a studious twelve year old girl. She stood out both because of her beauty and academic achievements. Sara had apparently been bullied by one of her classmates who according to her had some jealousy issues. The girl who was bullying Sara had previously cut her hair while sitting behind her in class. The young bully had also poured ink on Sara's clothing and took one of her books and damaged it. Sara had tried to talk to the bully to no avail and she told her mother about the incident on numerous occasions. Sara's mother had contacted the school and talked to the principal and one of the teachers but the harassment continued. Her mother tried repeatedly to contact the bully's mother and when she finally did contact her she responded by telling her, "I work two jobs and I don't have time for children's mess."

After about four months of none stop harassment, Sara had all she could stand. One day the bully decided to cut off another piece of her hair while sitting behind her in the class room. When she grabbed her hair Sara stood up and hit her with a book. A fight ensued and some of the children in class helped the teacher break up the fight. Sara was escorted to the principal's office crying. The bully was sent to the nurse to examine the knot on her head. The principal reminded Sara of the no tolerance fighting rule. Sara pointed out how she had come to the principal's office for help and had not received any. The principal ignored her. No one seemed to care that Sara had a 3.5 grade point average and perfect attendance.

The police were called and Sara tried to explain how she had been bullied for months. She also tried to explain to the police how she had tried to get help from the school authorities and was ignored. About thirty minutes later two police officers came into the principal's office and immediately the principal got up from his chair and went into another room with the officers. After about five minutes the officers returned to the principal's office the lady police officer had handcuffs in her hand. She asked Sara to stand up and told her, "you are under arrest for aggravated battery, turn around and place your hand behind you," As Sara did as she was told by the police, she felt the cold hard handcuffs being placed on her. Sara was frightened out of her mind. She repeatedly told the police that she had told the bully to stop messing with her but she would not, she told about had how she had gone to the teacher and principal and no one would help her. The police began reading her Miranda Rights while ignoring her request "you have the right to remain silent, you have a right to an attorney, and anything you say can and will be used against you...."

She was escorted from the school and placed in a police car she she was so hurt and embarrassed. The police refused to listen and assault charges were filed against Sara. Sara was process through the juvenile system and given a hearing date about a month from the time she was charged with aggravated battery. Before leaving the court room Sara was approached by a representative of the district attorney's office. She was informed of a program whereby she could attend classes and counseling and the charge would not be placed on her record.

Sara was very pleased to hear that that was a way to keep this information from being placed on her record. Sara had plans for her life which included going to law school after attending college. She knew that a criminal charge would hinder her from getting into the college or university that she wanted to attend.

Sara quickly agreed to taking the classes and counseling to avoid having a charge of aggravated battery on her criminal record. She breathed a sigh of relief knowing that her future would not be jeopardized by this unfortunate incident. The representative from the District attorney's office set up an appointment for her to come in and do the paperwork necessary to get into the program. Sara was so excited about the program when the Assistant District Attorney dropped the bomb. She told Sara to get into this Juvenile Diversion Program required a fee of $250.00. Sara's excitement soon turned to sorry. She did not have a job, her mother was on disability and her father was laid off work for the past eight months and his unemployment would soon be running out.

Sara left that court house with a whole different attitude about America's justice system. She wondered how could a system be called a justice system when in actuality it's just the opposite. Her hopes and admirations of being an attorney are gone because now she is a convicted felon. She is now one of the millions of African Americans who are unjustly criminalized by the legal system each year, myself included. Sara will not be able to get a federal job, many professional licenses will not be available to her, her voting right rights will be affected, many colleges and universities will not accept her and the list goes on and on.

These tactics are used to enslave and improvise those that the "good ole boys" see as a threat to their authority. Many judges bring with them to the bench their racist attitudes and hatred of minorities and the poor and use the court as a tool to practice their racism. Corrupt judges understand that laws like Pierson versus Ray will cover up their evil and protect them from exposured, to liability and punishment.

SYSTEMATIC DISENFRANCHISING OF MINORITY YOUTH

There have been many studies done to find out whether there is a disproportionate number of minority youth (in Louisiana primarily African American youth) being charged with crimes and processed through the legal system. Although most already know the answer; it looks good to the public to spend a little money in the form of a governmental grant to research this question of why so many African American youth are being charged and processed through the legal system. Under the freedom of information act, I acquired some of the research that had been done in some of the larger parishes in Louisiana on this issue. Many parishes didn't brother to keep records on this issue. The disparity between Whites and Blacks in the correctional system is nothing short of mind boggling.

The message being sent at each level of the Louisiana legal system is one of preparing African Americans for the correctional system, especially Black men. Starting at an early age the legal system brands Black men with a criminal record. This tactic will keep Black men unemployed and push them into a cycle of hopelessness, depression, anger and criminal activity. Part of the strategic plan of the penal and correctional institutions includes the built in mechanism of genocide of African American men and minority youth at a young age. I can hear you saying how ludicrous that sounds!! Now ask yourself why most states budgets include more money for prisons than colleges and universities. Let's apply a little logic and see if we can find the answer.

When young men are locked away with other young men at the height of their sexuality, it breeds a culture of homosexuality. Many men who enter into prison at an early age have their first sexual encounter with another male. Many of these men become spiritually and physically attracted to other men. These relationship lead to a loss of natural affection, broken families, absent fathers and men who cannot be committed to a woman in marriage. This culture produces large dysfunctional and fragmented families whose children are used to fill up jails and prisons. The statistics shows the tender of disparity in the treatment of African Americans in the correctional system of many of the large parishes in Louisiana.

THE BUSINESS OF THE JUSTICE SYSTEM

You may by now be asking yourself, "what do these things have to do with the American Justice Systems?" Let me tell you. To understand how anything operates you must first know it's genesis or origin to get a comprehensive picture of the complete operation. In studying or discussing the Louisiana Justice System there are several questions you might ask. Why does the poorest state in America have one of the largest prison populations? Better yet, why does this state with so many natural resources have so much proverty? Louisiana is probably one of a handful of states in America that could survive totally on its' own without any help from any other state or nation. Louisiana has tropical weather at least nine months out of the year. Louisiana has a vast amount of timber and fertile farm Land. Louisiana is the natural gas capital of America. This state has huge oil reserves and access to the Gulf of Mexico which allows it access to a massive seafood markets. Louisiana should be one of the richest states in the union but instead it is number one in poverty, has one of the worst education systems in America, leads the country in cancer, and has one of the highest rates of HIV/ AIDS infection and some of the most dilapidated highways in the country. Pre Katrina you were more likely to be killed in New Orleans than Iraq or Beruit Lebanon. For years New Orleans led the country in murders and HIV/AID infections. Why is this state so far behind and dysfunctional?

It is to the advantage of the power broker or those who are in control of the money and property to maintain a subclass or a system of second class citizens. You see this vividly on the African continent with the apartheid government that existed prior to Nelson Mandela taking office in South Africa. Those that were the landlord used the Willie Lynch theory to control and dominate Black South Africans for decades. This same system was used in America just not as obvious as South Africa.

When slavery was abolished slave masters had to figure out how to maintain their status quo without breaking the law. After all you could no longer chain slaves who refused to work for nothing. So what do the slave masters do now that they must pay the once slave. Many freed slaves remained on Louisiana plantations because they could not understand the concept of freedom. Without land or education what was he going to do? Change is one of the most difficult things in the world to do. Empirical data shows that beliefs that are irrational and neurotic learned early in life persist. The absence of reinforcement does not necessarily result in the extinction or elimination of a bad attitude or behavior. Although the behavior itself is not reinforced, the individual persists in the reinforcement of these early learned behaviors through a reindoctrination process that includes him telling himself how unworthy and no good he or she is. So he continues to behave irrationally because of his illogical thoughts about himself. Since all of the people that the slave saw in power were White men, many assumed that that was the way it was supposed to be, especially those born into slavery. Most slaves believed themselves to be inferior and never challenged the racist system. Some would even fight other slaves who dared to demand equal rights and pay.

Most of the agriculture in the southern United States during the early 19th century was dedicated to growing one crop cotton. Most of the cotton crop was grown on large plantations that used black slave labor. Slavery was an economic necessity in Louisiana and most of the south and was quickly institutionalized as a matter of law. Plantations often became gathering points for people in Mississippi towns. This was primarily because they were self-contained settlements. The plantation owner could provide food, shelter, and clothing for his family from the products of the plantation. Moreover, plantations often included hunting and riding grounds for the entertainment of the owner and visitors. Throughout the American Civil War (1861-1865), blacks working as slaves on plantations in the southern United States produced the food and supplies that sustained the Confederate army.

UNPUBLISHED JUDGMENTS

When attorneys file motions requesting the judge to do a specify thing they normally attach an order with all the detail of the request for the judge to sign. For example and attorney may request the judge to order a party to a paternity suit to give a DNA sample. The attorney making the request will attach an order with all of the details of the request in the order for the judge to sign. If the judge agrees he simply signs the order and copies are given by the requesting attorney to all parties of the case. The attorney may send it certified mail or have the sheriff or some other law enforcement agency to serve upon the parties the judgment signed by the judge. Some judges do not allow attorneys to write their judgments they prefer to write their own judgments signed them and distribute them to all parties themselves.

Those of us who have experienced civil trials are familiar with judgments. The judgment is a written document that is sometimes prepared by the judge but most often prepared by the prevailing attorney. Judgments first got my attention in a case that in Ouachita Parish Louisiana Van

Van was the plaintiff and the District attorney and Sheriff of Ouachita parish where the defendants. This case was filed in federal court because of the racism and cronyism that usually prevails within the district courts in the state of Louisiana although the federal courts are not much better, it is often better to try to file a case in the federal courts rather than to trust the District Courts where the good ole boy network and political agenda are so very prevalent.

Allow me to give you a little background as to the case that was filed in the federal courts against the District Attorney and Sheriff of Ouachita Parish. In Louisiana unlike the forty nine of the other states in the United States, we have the unique distinguish of naming our political property divisions of land. Whereas most states refer to their divisions as counties, in Louisiana we refer to them as parishes. This is due in part to the largely French culture in the state and the great influence of the Catholic Church. The only other states that do not have counties are New York which has boroughs and Alaska which has provinces.

The setting is in Monroe, Louisiana where a young Black man by the name of Van grew up in the rural area. Van began working for Allstate Insurance Company about two years after being honorably discharged from the United States Army. Shortly after being discharged from the Army Van began to work in retail at a store in Monroe Louisiana namely Montgomery Wards.

After working at Montgomery wards for a short period of time approximately three months Van discovered that he was being scouted by Allstate insurance company representatives. While on the sales floor at Montgomery Ward engaged doing his usual activities of trying to sell televisions and stereo equipment, he was approached by a young man by the name of Ken. Van notice for several days this young man had come to his department asking questions about the equipment that he sold at Montgomery Ward and engaged in a lot of small talk. After the third day of coming by his department and engaging in small talk he finally introduced himself as a district manager for Allstate Insurance Company. He informed Van that Allstate was interested in hiring him as an agent. Van was a little excited about the offer because Van was very tired of selling televisions and stereos. Van would have a good week and sell ten or twelve units and the next week seem as though seven or eight were returned. After a few weeks however Van was hired by Allstate and was beginning my training. Many of the staff at Allstate made a big deal out of the fact that Van was the second African American hired by Allstate Insurance Company in the state of Louisiana. Some liked to joke about the fact that the first one was fired for theft. Van worked for Allstate about eight years and made a decent living, but nothing to brag about.

Louisiana prior to 1978 was one of few states that did not require individuals to have automobile insurance to operate a motor vehicle. The state of Louisiana passed a mandatory insurance law requiring that all owners of motor vehicles must carry on a mobile insurance. Van began to see this law as an excellent opportunity to become self-employed. Van found some property within the city limits about four miles where he worked as an Allstate agent. After finding the property his next biggest dilemma was finding the funds to purchase the property. After doing extensive research he found that the governor had a program to loan seed money to small businesses. Van contacted the governor's office and was directed to a lady who was the director or the department that supply seed money to small businesses. Van was given a loan application to fill out to begin the loan process for the seed money. After about two months Van was given approval for seed money that would be insured by the state of Louisiana.

Van remember thinking what a wonderful deed for a Republican governor to do to assist minorities and setting up small businesses. In Louisiana Republicans are not known for their friendship of minority persons. This became evident when Van went to the bank who would be the primary lender.

Van was assigned a young man of approximately the same age as Van was to manage my account. This young man made it apparent that he did not care very much for Van as a patron from the onset and made it very obvious. As much as he disliked the fact that Van was getting a bank loan he could not prevent it. Van received a $50,000 state guaranteed loan to start his business. Van was somewhat frightened from the beginning because this would be a new venture into unchartered waters for him. Van purchased a piece of property within the inner city and an abandoned service station. Van remodel the service station and hung his sign letting everyone know that he was in business. Van began to get lots of business almost immediately. Although business was very good Van soon discovered that he would need to have additional sources of income other than just automobile insurance which was his primary source of income.

      One day while sitting at his desk pondering what would be the best way to get additional income an acquaintance that Van will call Tom came by his office whom Van had met at a party some months ago. He began to talk about the insurance business and he informed me that he was also in the insurance business but not in the automobile insurance. Tom informed me that he was in the bail bonding business. As he talked about the bail bonding business Van became very interested because Van knew that the majority of the persons whom needed bail bonds were African Americans. Van also discovered that he already had the license that Van needed to add that service to my company. They talked for several hours and the more they talked the more interests Van gained. Van saw an excellent opportunity to add a new service to his existing business that would be very profitable and give him the income that he needed to keep his business afloat and in the black. After a few weeks at a few telephone calls to various bail bond companies Van had found and secured a company that Van could write bail bonds through and that gave him an excellent commission. When Tom heard that Van was in the bail bonding business he approached him about working for him. They talked and came to an agreement whereby he could make an excellent commission and Van would make a good profit as well. After a few weeks he informed his friends about the deal that Van had given him. Two other agents who were writing bail bonds for Van's competition came to his office and stated they would like to work for his agency as well. Van signed them both to a contract and therefore very long they were the largest bail bond agency and the three surrounding parishes.

This angered many of the judges and the law enforcement officials who were a part of the racist,' good ole boy', network. They did not like the idea of a black bail bonding company with black agents having that much influence on the legal system. After being in business for about three months we had the majority of the bail bond business in three parishes. The bail bondman in Louisiana usually set the court dates for the appearance of the person charged. This gives the bail bondsmen a lot of influence in the way the court system operates.

His brother had lost his job months prior to Van getting into the bail bonding business. He had applied with the sheriff's office for employment but was turned down. He came to work at Van agency as a bail bondsman and was doing well financially. He knew the city well and knew how to deal with the criminal element of society better than Van. When the sheriff discovered that Van's brother was working for Van's agency his interest in hiring him changed. He asked his brother to come in for an interview and lie detector test. Most of the lie detector test was questions about Van and his agency. The sheriff wanted to know was Van dealing in drugs or any illegal activity. Van had never been investigated, accused or engaged in any illegal activities. Van knew then that the "good ole boy" system was at work trying to destroy his business. This became even more evident when Van decided to extend his bail bond business into West Monroe. To get approval in West Monroe Van had to go through a devout racist judge whom I will call Judge Baylor. Van called his office and set up an appointment to see him. Upon entering his office he did not try to hide his contempt and hatred. He wanted to know what company did Van represent and the history of the company. Van informed him that all of that information could be gotten from the insurance commissioner and show him a copy of the insurance commission registry book which he took and refuse to give back. Judge Baylor then stated that he would have to talk to the commissioner of insurance himself the registry was not sufficient evidence of the stability of the company to write bond in his court even though the company was a nationally known company. He held Van up for months before finally allowing his agency to write bonds in his city court. Of course this is both illegal and unfair but in Louisiana it is the way things are done with the "good ole boy" network.

Many covert attempts were used to try to destroy Van's business. Van got several anonymous calls in early morning hours from person wanting him to come to the jail and bail out Mexican, These men and sometime women were in this country illegal and used as what is referred to in the dope smuggling world as "mules." These anonymous callers would request that Van come to the parish jail and bond these people out. Van knew better than to bond these peoples out of jail. Van knew as soon as their feet hit the ground that they would be running for the Mexican border.

After a few months of prosperity the devil began to rear his ugly head. About one o'clock midnight Van received a call from an elderly man from Mississippi who was stopped by the parish Sheriff Deputy while patrolling the highway for drunk drivers. The elderly man was stopped by the deputy and found to be driving while intoxicated. Van received a call from the man stating that he was in the parish jail and wanted to be bonded out. He stated that his bond was fifteen hundred dollars. He was being charged with reckless driving and driving while intoxicated. The reckless driving bond was five hundred dollars, for which he would need fifty dollars cash. The driving while intoxicated bond was one thousand dollars for which he would need one hundred cash. After explaining all of the details of his arrest the gentleman stated to him that he had no cash in his possession. Van explained to the gentleman that bail bonds required cash payments only. He informed Van that he could write him a check and wait until the check had cleared the bank. He also informed Van that this would be a benefit to him since he had some medical conditions and had no insurance and while incarcerated the state could examine him and give him the medicine that he needed without cost to him. Van understood his dilemma and agree to except a check and send it for collection and after the funds were deposited in his account bail him out of jail. It took about four days for the check to clear the bank and deposit the cash in his account. While waiting for the check to clear the bank his daughter was searching for the elderly man and discovered that he was in the Ouachita parish jail. She drove approximately two hours from Mississippi to the jail and bonded him out with a cash bond. Van discovered this on the fourth day after the check had cleared the bank. Van came to the jail to bond the gentleman out and discovered that he had already been bonded out by his daughter. This was a Friday and all the following Monday Van was notified by the elderly gentleman that he would no longer need my services. He gave Van his address to send his refund and he did so. About a week later Van received a certified letter in the mail. From my experience in the past certified letters are usually not good news. Van went to the post office to retrieve a certified letter and discovered that it was from the Ouachita parish Sheriff's office. Van immediately opened the letter and began to read it. To his surprise the sheriff was informing him that he was banned from riding bail bonds in the Ouachita parish jail. He alleged that he had received reports that Van had taken money for bail bonds that he did not make. He went on to state that this was a violation of his department's policy and could be viewed as criminal. Van was not overly concerned although it was very shocking and he wondered where the sheriff could have gotten such misinformation. He returned to his office and immediately placed a call to the sheriff's secretary to set up an appointment to talk to him. The secretary was very cordial and gave him an appointment date about two days away.

    Van went to sheriff's office and noticed the secretary and two other deputies standing just outside of his office. Van introduced himself to the secretary and told her he had an appointment to see the sheriff.

She proceeded to the sheriff's office and return very shortly. At that time the two deputies who were waiting by the secretary desk entered the sheriff's office. A few minutes later he opened the door and told Van to come in and have a seat. Van immediately noticed that his tone was not very cordial. Van assumed that this would be a very short visit and that he would be able to explain to him that he had made a mistake and everything would return to normal as far as his business relationship with his office.

Upon entering the sheriff's office he noticed one deputy stood to his side while the other deputy stood just to the rear of Van's chair. Van found this to be very intimidating and threatening and it made him somewhat angry. He told Sheriff Godwin about the letter that he had sent me and stated that he was misinformed. Van told the sheriff that he had never taken anyone's money and not provided them with the bond. The sheriff had a smirk on his face as though he didn't take the conversation seriously. He asked about the elderly gentleman that Van had sent the check for collection before bonding him out of jail. He began to explain the situation and he interrupted Van saying, "I don't want to hear it, just don't write bonds in my jail unless I tell you." Van got so angry he felt like punching him; he had donated money to his campaign and considered him a friend but his loyalty was to the "good ole boys" racist. He knew then that this was all part of a set up. The parish jail was the large source of the bail bonding business. They knew if this source of revenue was eliminated that it would soon put Van and his other agents out of business, this was the game plan.

Van had several friends that were lawyers so he began making calls to get legal advices on how to get his bonding rights restored in the Parish Jail. It was urgent that he get his bonding rights restored since the parish jail was the major source of income. All of the major felony charges were processed through the parish jail. The sheriff and his cronies knew this also. They knew if neither he nor his agents were allowed to write bonds in the parish jail that he would soon be out of business.

Unfortunate for Van most of his attorney friend were cowards. They were afraid to take on the sheriff department in a law suit. The sheriff office is usually the agent of process; meaning they are the agency that service the legal document upon the party to suit and other legal matters for attorneys. They were afraid that the sheriff might harass them if they filed suit and not properly serve their litigants.

As fate would have it one of his attorney friends was doing some research on another case and ran across a case exactly like Van's. The suit was based upon a sheriff who was interfering with a bail bondman doing business in the parish jail, (Cormier Versus Vidrine 491 So. 2d 397 (LA. 3d Cir. 1986). Van said to himself thank" God now there is no way they can get out of this injustice that they have done to me." The cases were so similar that they appeared to be the same case. Attorney use previous cases that have gone before judges and the final judgment of those cases to show cause why they should prevail on their case, these are referred to as precedence. Therefore an attorney or person present a case similar to their case and can show that the court ruled in their favor is supposed to win a favorable judgment. Again here is where the "good ole boys" step in and change the rule.

Van was very excited and knew that his victory was simply a matter of time. After contacting several attorneys to no avail, he decided to contact the Civil Rights Commission after much "run around" he was finally given a "right to sue." he did not understand at that point why he needed a "right to sue" he thought that anyone who had been done an injustice could sue and had a right to do so. Van soon found out that was not the case. Many judges for several reason some justifiable and some not will prevent a case from going to court. Many times a judge may want to help out a friend, so he will dismiss the case before trial usually on the motion of a summary judgment from one of the parties. This would cause the non- prevailing party to pay more money in the form of attorney fees, court cost and time to do an appeal to a higher court. Most of the time the case will end with a summary judgment because of the expense involved. The odds of getting a lower court overturned even when the judges are wrong are very low. The Civil Rights Commission after reviewing a complaint of discrimination can issue a "right to sue." This prevents dishonest and corrupt judges from dismissing cases on summary judgment before trial.

Van had little or no money to fight this case, all he had was his belief in God and a determination that he was not going to be abused by the legal system like his ancestors. He spent many days and nights researching law books and in the library. It seemed as though fate was in his corner. A lady that he knew was at the sheriff's office handling some business matters and had over heard him say that Van probably wouldn't make it to court because he was hiding from law enforcement. She was so shocked at the conversation that she called Van as soon as she returned home to tell him to be very alert. He took her advice seriously because another sheriff department employee whom he knew well and worked close with the sheriff had warned him to be careful and try not to travel much at night because she knew of a case where the sheriff had setup an accident for the son of one of his adversaries who threaten to expose illegal activities within the department. After weeks of research Van manage to put together a lawsuit for the Federal Courts. He filed the suit and sent the defendants a set of interrogatories. Interrogatories are questions either party can submit to gather information that they would like to use in their case. Interrogatories must be relevant to the case and not used as harassment or stalling tactic. Once the party receives the interrogatories he/she has a certain amount of days to answer them or a motion to "compel discovery" may be filed in the court by the moving party. The court will then sat a court date to determine whether the judge will sign the motion to compel discovery (answer the questions) or not. The judge may also issues sanctions in the form of monetary compensation to the moving party. The issuing party must certify to the court that the interrogatories were served upon the opposing party. They are sometime served by mailing them in the U.S. Mail or by having the sheriff or some other law enforcement agency to serve them.

Interrogatories were served upon the sheriff in a legal manner. After the time for the answer to the interrogatories had expired without hearing from the sheriff a motion to compel was filed. Many attorneys believe that they do not abide by the law when it comes to "pro se litigates." He waited a few days after the due dates for the answer to the interrogatories and received no answers. He filed a motion to compel discovery and had court to serve the request upon the sheriff. The judge set a court date to hear the motion. The motion was done properly and the judge couldn't find an excuse to deny Van's motion. The judge granted the motion and ordered the attorney to answer his interrogatories. This angered the attorney but he compel with order.

    The defense attorney really didn't think he knew enough about the law to file a motion to compel discovery and he probably thought that the judge would patronize him and play the harassment game since Van was not an attorney. But to both of our surprise he awarded him the motion to compel discovery and order the defendants to their surprise to answer the interrogatories. After months of discovery between Van, the sheriff, and district attorney's office it became time for the pretrial order.

    Judges and lawyers dislike seeing persons file a suit in "proper person or Pro Se", that is to file without having or paying a lawyer; they deem it a threat to their pocket book first and foremost. They believe that if the judges allow persons to prevail in court without a lawyer then lawyers, incomes will be diminished. To avoid having lawyers lose money many judges will harass pro se litigates to discourage them from representing themselves. They use the old phrase "the person whose lawyer is himself lawyer is a fool." But little is said about the person who consistently pay lawyers who do nothing is a fool. I have seen on numerous occasions where people spend thousands of dollars and all the lawyer do is write letters that were "cut and paste" from previous letters. This is a tactic used to supposedly justify running up a legal bill every month until you can't pay and then he goes to court and ask for a motion to be dismissed from the case.

Pretrial order is an agenda of what each party plans to present at the trial. All experts, witnesses, exhibits and anything one plans to use at the trial. It's not at all like the television programs where the attorney bring into court this surprise witness or evidence and wins the case.

After about a month of preparing and filing the pretrial order Van was given a pretrial hearing. The purpose of the pretrial hearing is for the judge to see if a compromise can be had and avoid the expense of a trial.

The judge knew that all of the evidence was in Van's favor and there was no way he could *LEGALLY* rule in favor of the defendant. Judge Walter reluctantly told the defendants to reach a settlement with Van. In about a week Van got this letter stating that they would give him three thousand dollars without admitting any liabilities as a final settlement. Three thousand dollars equal to about two weeks income from the bonding business at the most. So what they wanted to give Van was about two week's income for putting him out of business. Of course his answer was not no but *"hell no."* Van sent them a counter offer of eight hundred thousand dollars. He wanted them to know that he was not going to settle for "chicken feed", and go away. Van never expected them to give him the eight hundred dollars that he had demanded; but at this point in his life it really didn't matter. His main goal was to expose these devils for who and what they really are. Of course he never heard back from them on the counter offer. After a couple of week a trial date was set. In setting the trial date Van omitted one very important issue, *a trial by jury.* Van knew that Judge Donald Walters was going to try to help the defense as much as he could because Van was not represented by an attorney and would not settle for the cheap settlement offered by the defense. Far too many judges are more concerned about lawyers getting rich rather than seeing justice prevail.

    Van attempted to amend his pre- trial order to include a jury trial but was meant with fierce resistance for the defense attorney. They wanted to keep the proceeding as quiet and unnoticed as possible. He tried very hard to persuade the judge to amend his petition to have a trial by jury but to no avail. This is the reason for the "right to sue order" issued by the civil rights commission. If he did not have the right to sue order from the civil rights commission he probably would not have gotten to a trial at all. The judge would have simply dismissed it on a motion from the defense. He also wanted to add a keywitness to the list. This motion was also denied by the judge. Judge Donald Walter did all he could to help the defense case.

Finally the trial date arrived. Van came to court with two big boxes of evidence. Not only did he prove that the sheriff actions were based upon racial prejudice but he presented evidence to show that the sheriff had no power or authority to act in the capacity that he did. All of the evidence and witnesses fell on deaf ears. It was obvious that Judge Walters had already made up in his mind that the defense would win.

So after all the pretense of a trial by Judge Walters he finally did what he knew he would from the beginning; rule in the defendant favor. Van ask for an appeal to his decision. The judge became so mad that he broke his writing pen.

Van filed an appeal showing all of his evidence and the precedence that was already set in this case. He received a reply that literally knocked him off his feet. Had someone told him that the federal court system was as corrupt as he found it to be he would have told them that they were a liar. The federal appeal court is where one would think that they would have a chance of a fair trial; not if you're Black. You will get a fair trial if they are trying to put you in prison and that's about the only time. After the façade of a trial was over and Judge Donald Walter made his ruling. He ruled in the defendant favor without any explanation, since there was no legal basis for his ruling.

He filed his appeal as required making sure everything was done properly and on time. After about three months he received a ruling that that was totally obsurd and ludicrous. The ruling stated that the district judge ruling was based on his bad attitude. I have yet to see that statue ordinance or law anywhere in the constitution or in any law book. They were referring to the statement that he had made in his brief that it was almost impossible in civil proceedings for a Black man to get a favorable decision against a White man for monetary damages. The irony of the decision is that both the district and appeal court proved him right.

To add insult to injury the decision came with bold print that this is an **unpublished decision**. This is a systematic way to cover up corrupt and illegal activity of the court without the public's knowledge. The unpublished decisions cannot be used as precedence in other cases. This is why the courts keep them hid from the public. Of course he sent a motion requesting that the decision be published but never heard back from the court.

SYSTEMATIC RACISM

A lot of injustice in this country is based on economics. When few people have jobs and the majority of those with jobs pay very little money it creates an economic stimulus. By that I mean that the value of the dollar is very high when there are very few dollars to go around. It is the same principle of supply and demand. When the demand of something is great and the supply is low the value and price of that item is high. When the supply is great and the demand is low the item becomes very inexpensive.

Did you ever wonder why a Black person can go to the BMW or Mercedes Bentz auto dealership at 9 a.m. in the morning and by 5 p.m. the same day can drive away with a $100,000 car. All that person needs is a little credit and a job. Sometimes he doesn't need a job if he has enough cash money. Now that same person can go to a realtor to buy a house at 9 a.m. and he will be fortunate to get in the house by the next month. Now they will tell you the reason for the disparity of time is due to title work and legal details involved in transferring of land. But the truth is the big car is something that will keep you in proverty and the house and land is something that will enrich you. Also the car will help to keep the rich richer and the poor even poorer.

Unemployment is maintained in the United States at an average of about 7 percent. This figure is usually acceptable. Fewer people with dollars make the dollar more valuable. This is why five percent of the people in this country own eighty percent of the wealth. These are the people who fund political campaigns. In return the politicians make law to insure that they maintain their wealth. Although the people ultimately elect their representative in government their decisions are usually based upon the billboards along the highways the radio advertising the newspaper advertisements and mainly the television advertisements. In Louisiana alone it cost as much to run for the governor's office as it does for the president of the United States. Those in power keep tight hold on who comes to power.

Doing the nineteen sixties and seventies African American began to rebel and threaten a violent revolution if the government did not do something about the racial injustice that was so prevalent in this country. Many minorities were fed up with fighting wars for freedoms that they did not have. Louisiana, Mississippi and many other southern states were known for killing Black soldiers for wearing the United State military uniform. President Kennedy began the move to pass some law to correct some of the injustices although many carried little or no punishment when not compiled with. After the death of President Kennedy, President Johnson passed some major legislation to help stop racial discrimination and injustices. Most of those laws were short lived after President Johnson's tenure as president. President Ronald Wilson Reagan came to power and removed most of the teeth from the discrimination laws. President Ronald Reagan put laws in place stating that "one must prove the intent to discriminate and show racial prejudice". Of course this is understandable coming from a man who states that he did not know that racial discrimination existed in the United States. This act of President Reagan was done to maintain the economic disparities between Black and other minorities and Whites. He appointed a few Blacks to office and used them as rubber stamps. I recall the big scandal at the Department of Urban Development supposedly headed by an African American that was appropriately nick named "Silent Sam." When millions of dollars disappeared from his department he had no idea where is was or what was going on within the department that he was supposed to have been heading. Yet because he was named as the head of the department all the blame fell on him.

Many Blacks and other minorities believe and often do sell their souls to gain a political office. No matter how good of a guy you may be and how well your intensions are unless you can get the corporate dollars you will more often than not loss your bid for public office.

Whether one likes President Obama or not, you'll have to admit he has got to be one of the smartest men in America. He used a very unique approach to fund raising which was largely seen as unorthodox to say the least. He chose not to take the Government funding for his campaign but rather getting the small contributions from grass root peoples; five, ten, twenty dollars. To most of the countries' surprise he raised more money than most of the presidential candidates using this method.

This method of fund raising gave President Obama some independence from the powers that be. After all I have to admit we still go by the golden rule, "whoever has the gold makes the rules." Even with the independence from big business he still has to deal with a congress that appear more concern about making him look bad that correcting our countries problem. Many of them seem to have the Russ Lumbar syndrome. Russ a popular talk show host that many who rode the "short bus" listen to daily, state that all he is concerned about is Obama failing.

I remember hearing a quote long ago which says "be careful how you choose your enemies for they are the ones you became most like." I wonder for a long time what that statement meant, but the saying stayed in my spirit. I soon found out what it meant after reading a speech made by a famous slave consultant by the name of Willie Lynch. Here is a copy of the speech he wrote to slave owners.

THE SPEECH
By
Willie Lynch

Gentlemen:

I greet you here on the banks of the James River in the year of our Lord, one thousand seven hundred and twelve. First, I shall thank you, the Gentlemen of the Colony of Virginia for bringing me here. I am here to help you solve your problems with the slaves. Your invitation reached me on my modest plantation in the West Indies where I have experimented with some of the newest and still the oldest methods for control of slaves. Ancient Rome would envy us if my program is implemented. As our boat sailed south on the James River, named for our illustrious King, whose version of the Bible we cherish, I saw enough to know that your problem is not unique. While Rome used cords of wood as crosses for standing human bodies along its old highways in great numbers, you are here using the tree and rope on occasion.

I caught whiff of a dead slave hanging from a tree a couple of miles back. You are not only losing valuable stock by hangings, you are having uprisings, slaves are running away, your crops are sometimes left in the field too long for maximum profit, you suffer occasional fires, your animals are killed. Gentlemen, you know what you problems are; I do not need to elaborate, I am not here to enumerate your problems, I am here to introduce you to a method of solving them.

In my bag here, I Have a fool-proof method for controlling your black slaves. I guarantee every one of you that if installed correctly it will control the slaves for at least 300 years. My method is simple and members of your family or any overseer can use it.

I have outlined a number of differences among the slaves and I have taken these differences and make them bigger. I use fear, distrust, and envy for control purposes. These methods have worked on my modest plantation in the West Indies and it will work throughout the South. Take this simple little list of differences, think about them. On top of my list is "age," but it is there only because it starts with an "a"; the second is "color (or shade)"; there is intelligence, size, sex, size of plantation, status on plantation, attitude of owner, whether the slaves live in the valley or on a hill, east, west, north, south, have fine hair or coarse hair, or is tall or short. Now that you have a list of differences, I shall give you an outline of action, but before that, I shall assure you that distrust is stronger than trust, and envy is stronger than adulation, respect or admiration.

The black slave after receiving this indoctrination shall carry on and will become self-refueling and self-generating for hundreds of years, maybe thousands.

Don't forget you must pitch the old black vs the young black male and the young black male vs the old black male. You must use the dark skin slaves vs the light skin slaves and the light skin slaves vs the dark slaves. You must also have your white servants and overseers distrust ALL blacks, but it is necessary they trust and depend on us. They must love, respect, and trust ONLY us.

Gentlemen, these kits are your control; use them. Have your wives and children use them, never miss an opportunity. My plan is guaranteed, and the good thing about this plan is that if used **INTENSELY** for one year the slaves themselves will remain perpetually distrustful.

Thank you gentlemen,

Willie Lynch
Willie Lynch
1712

The troubled ghetto child response is mostly due to years of conditioning, whether it be the results of a dysfunctional family, television, radio or newspaper. The Black slave was conditioned to be subservient through classical conditioning. The conditioning process consisted of both rewards and punishment.

Mostly punishment was administered when the desired response was not received by the slave's master. Systems of indoctrination were set up and incorporated into the social as well as the legal system to enforce this conditioning. Willie Lynch in his address to slave owners in the 1700's eloquently articulated this philosophy of indoctrination. He points out that, "distrust is greater than trust, envy is greater than admiration and hatred would overcome love," (Lynch, 1712). These were the mechanisms of change that Lynch used. He instructed the slave owners to not kill rebellious slaves but pit them against each other by favoring the lighter skin over the darker skin, the younger against the older, and the woman against the man. He advised them to instill in them that the master and his people are the only people that can be trusted. Lynch points out that after only a few years of this type of indoctrination that the slaves themselves would become self-refueling and carry on the desired behavior for decades without further training.

These are the same tactics that the Dutch used in Rwanda to colonize the people and instill self-hatred, better known as divide and conquer. The Dutch chose one tribal group and gave them the better and easier jobs and gave the other group the menial and low paying jobs based on nose size and facial futures. This instilled division and hatred among the tribes and while they fought each other the Dutch literally took possession of the country while supplying weapons and supplies to be used by the tribes to kill each other.

People have always sort how to enslave other peoples for economic purposes. It is much easier to sit under a tree and drink mint juleps while someone else raises your crops and do your manual labor. Colonization and slavery bring about some interesting question as to man relationship to each other. One of the main questions addressed by the followers of the theory of Darwinism is that only the strongest of a species shall survive. Darwinist have a basis belief that what is should be and what is not should not be. They are of the opinion, "if one can be conquered then one should be conquered. If one can be enslaved then one should be enslaved." If one chooses not believe in morals, integrity and character this theory could be applicable. My guess is that most people opinion of the Darwin theory depends on ones status in life or which side of the spectrum they resident; whether they are the conqueror or the conquered, the servant or the master, the lender or borrower, the landlord or the land less.

After the Civil War many Black in Louisiana were elected to powerful offices even the governor of Louisiana P.B. S. Pinchback a Black man served as governor for a very short time; one month four days to be exact. Mississippi had many elected African Americans which only lasted a short time and ended after a few month by Klan who raid the political establishments killing and uproot the African American politicians. Many promises were made to help the African American family but very few of these promises were ever kept. The most famous and talked about was the forty acres and a mule promised to free slaves.

Fourty acres and a mule was a practice in 1865 of providing arable land to African American former slaves who became free as Union armies occupied areas of the Confederacy, especially in Sherman's March. Maj. General William T. Sherman's January 16, 1865 Special Field Orders No. 15 provided for the land, and some of the recipients received from the Army mules for use in plowing as well; the combination was widely recognized as providing a sound start for a family farm. Fourty acres is a standard size for rural land, being a sixteenth of a section, or a quarter section, under the Public Land Survey System used on land settled after 1785.

Sherman's orders specifically allocated "the islands from Charleston, south, the abandoned rice fields along the rivers for thirty miles back from the sea, and the country bordering the St. Johns river Florida".

After the assassination of President Abraham Lincoln, his successor, Andrew Johnson, revoked Sherman's Orders. It is sometimes mistakenly claimed that Johnson also vetoed the enactment of the policy as a federal statute (introduced as U.S. Senate Bill 60). In fact, the Freedmen's Bureau Bill which he vetoed made no mention of grants of land or mules. (Another version of the Freedmen's bill, also without the land grants, was later passed after Johnson's second veto was overridden.)

By June 1865, around 10,000 freed slaves were settled on 400,000 acres (160,000) in Georgia and South Carolina. Soon after, President Andrew Johnson reversed the order and returned the land to its white former owners. Because of this, the phrase has come to represent the failure of Reconstruction and the general public to assist African Americans.

Since the vast majority of the freed slaves were illiterate and were forbidden access to the Legal System the land was quickly taken and many of the freed slaves were killed or forced to be share croppers on their own land.

Share cropping soon became the primary vocation of the African American in Louisiana. Long days working in cane field, rice fields and cotton fields. Cotton was a very lucrative industry than required a large labor force. This was "quasi – slavery" and used as a tool to disenfranchising of a large segment of the America. Conditioning was an important fact in maintaining the new approach to control. Condition had to become both a cultural and a legal mechanism to be effective in controlling the large Negro population. Conditioning is seen in cults. They gave one a sense of their rightful place within society.

Classical conditioning is used by both Lynch and others to alter the behavior patterns of both humans and animals. To overcome the negative conditioning there must be a renewing of the mind. Paul tells us in the instruction book I call the Bible that we must dedicate our bodies and minds to God, "<u>I beseech you therefore brethren, by the mercies of God, that you present your bodies a living sacrifice, holy, acceptable unto God, which is your reasonable service. And be not conformed to this world: but be transformed by the renewing of your mind, that you may prove what is that good, and acceptable, and perfect will of God (Romans 12:2"</u>

Empirical data shows that beliefs that are irrational and neurotic learned early in life persist. The absence of reinforcement does not necessarily result in the extinction or elimination of a bad attitude or behavior. Although the behavior itself is not reinforced, the individual persists in the reinforcement of these early learned behaviors through a reindoctrination process that includes him telling himself how unworthy and no good he or she is. So he continues to behave irrationally because of his illogical thoughts about himself.

We find that the major goal of Christian doctrine and many other religions is to change the thought patterns. In the case of a drug abuser Christian doctrine is to address the thoughts that relate to meanings such as purpose, values and morals. Thoughts are very powerful and underestimated by most peoples. An example is to sit quietly and think about something and after a short time of thinking you will begin to verbalize out loud your thoughts. And that brings another little known human characteristic and that is that **words have power.** In school many children are taught "sticks and stones may break my bones but words cannot harm me." Children would be better taught that "loose lips sink battle ships." Nothing could be further from the truth, talk can kill you, and words have tremendous power. Doing biblical times when the king made a decree or edict; that is to make a law even he could not change it. The Bible tells us for one to be saved from sin that is to have salvation and eternal life one must believe in his heart and confess with his mouth. Nothing happens until something is said.

Government Conspiracy Theory

Many African American believe that the government constantly plans and implement ways to suppress African Americans. This is understandable given the United States record of terrorism against Blacks in both the north and south regions of this country.

Racism up and until about the late sixties made it almost impossible for a Black man to become rich legally. It is a strong held belief in many African American communities until this day that a Black man who has a successful business should maintain a low profile and stay out of site to avoid racist from taking his business. It is almost impossible even today for African American man to get a civil monetary award against a White person or business regardless of how much evidence he presents in court. This is from my own experience in Ouachita Parish Louisiana with Van Harvey D/B/A Harvey Bail Bonding versus Sheriff Laymon Godwin and District Attorney James Norris who conspired to close Van's bail bonding business.

Many African Americans as well as Whites think that the only way for an African American to get rich in this country is to do something illegal such as selling drugs or sell his soul to the powers that be.

I hear you saying this guy is some paranoid. Here's a typical example; a man who I will call Brown for privacy purpose. You will find hundred and thousands of Frank Brown's throughout urban American.

Brown was born in La Grange, North Carolina and raised in Greensboro, North Carolina. He claims that the incident that sparked his motivation to embark on a life of crime was witnessing his 12-year-old cousin's murder at the hands of the Ku Klux Klan, for apparently "reckless eyeballing" (looking at a Caucasian woman), in Greensboro, North Carolina. He drifted through a life of petty crime until one particular occasion when after a fight with a former employer he fled to New York on the advice of his mother. In Harlem he indulged in petty crime and pool hustling before he was taken under the wing of gangster Sammy Smith. Brown' connection to Johnson has since come under some doubt; he claimed to have been Johnson's driver for 15 years, although Johnson spent just five years out of prison before his death in 1968. According to Johnson's widow, much of the narrative that Brown claims as his actually belonged to another young hustler named Sam Walker, who lived with Johnson and his family and later betrayed him.

Criminal career

After Smith's death, Brown traveled around and came to the realization that to be successful he would have to break the monopoly that the Italian mafia held in New York. Traveling to Bangkok, Thailand, he eventually made his way to Jack's American Star Bar, an R&R hangout for black soldiers. It was here that he met former U.S. Army sergeant Leslie "Ike" Atkinson , a country boy from Goldsboro, North Carolina, who happened to be married to one of Brown' cousins. Brown is quoted as saying, "Ike knew everyone over there, every black guy in the Army, from the cooks on up."

When interviewed for a magazine article published

in 2000, Brown denied putting the drugs among the corpse of American soldiers. Instead he flew with a North Carolina carpenter to Bangkok and built furniture and shipped heroin back to the states.

However, Atkinson, nicknamed "Sergeant Smack" by the DEA, has said he shipped drugs in furniture, not casket. Whatever method he used, Brown smuggled the drugs into the country with this direct link from Asia. Brown said that he made 1 million per day selling drugs on 116TH Street though this was later discovered to be an exaggeration. Brown probably netted about half a Federal judge Sterling Johnson, who was special narcotics prosecutor in New York at the time of Brown' crimes, called Brown' operation "one of the most outrageous international dope-smuggling gangs ever, an innovator who got his own connections outside the U.S. and then sold the narcotics himself in the street." He had connections with the Five Families, holding an enormous monopoly on the heroin market in Manhattan. In an interview, Brown said, "I wanted to be rich. I wanted to be Donald Trump rich, and so help me God, I made it."

Brown only trusted relatives and close friends from North Carolina to handle his various heroin operations. Brown thought they were less likely to steal from him and be tempted by various vices in the big city. He stated his heroin, "Blue Magic", was 98-100% pure when shipped from Thailand. Brown has been quoted as saying that his worth was "something like $52 million", most of it in banks in the Cayman Islands. Added to this is "maybe 1,000 keys (kilograms), (2,200 pounds), of dope on hand" with a potential profit of no less than $300,000 per kilo (per 2.2lb)

This huge profit margin allowed him to buy property all over the country, including office buildings in Detroit, and apartments in Los Angeles and Miami. He also bought a several-thousand-acre ranch in North Carolina on which he ranged 300 head of Black Angus cattle, including a breeding bull worth $125,000.

Brown rubbed shoulders with the elite of the entertainment, politics, and crime worlds, stating later that he had met Howard Hughes at one of Harlem's best clubs in his day. Though he owned several mink and chinchilla coats and other accessories, Brown much preferred to dress casually and corporately so as not to attract attention to himself. He fathered seven children, including a daughter, Francine Brown-Sinclair, and a son, Frank Brown, Jr. When he was arrested in the mid-1970s, all of Brown' assets were seized.

"The properties in Chicago, Detroit, Miami, North Carolina, and Puerto Rico— they took everything. My lawyer told me they couldn't take the money in the offshore accounts, and I had all my money stored in the Cayman Islands. But that's BS; they can take it. Take my word for it. If you got something, hide it, 'cause they can go to any bank and take it. " — Frank Brown

Arrests and releases

After a long run of successful drug dealing it all starting coming to an end. In January 1975, Brown' house in Teaneck, New Jersey was raided by a task force consisting of 10 agents from Group 22 of the U.S. Drug Enforcement Agency and 10 New

York Police Department detectives attached to the Organized Crime Control Bureau (OCCB). In his house authorities found $584,683 in cash. He was later convicted of both Federal and New Jersey state drug violations. The following year he was sentenced to 70 years in prison. Once convicted, Brown provided evidence that led to more than 100 further drug-related convictions. For his safety in 1977, Brown and his family were placed in the witness protection program. In 1981, after 5 years in custody, his 40-year Federal term and 30-year state term were reduced to time served plus lifetime parole. In 1984 he was caught and convicted of trying to exchange one ounce of heroin and $13,000 for one kilogram of cocaine. He was defended by his former prosecutor Richie Roberts and received a sentence of seven years. He was released from prison in 1991.

Family

Brown married Julianna Brow, a homecoming queen from Puerto Rico (not Miss Puerto Rico as portrayed in the movie, American Gangster). The couple bought each other expensive gifts including a coat for which she paid $125,000 and another $40,000 cash for a matching hat. Brown wife Julie was also jailed for her role in her husband's criminal enterprise, spending five years behind bars. After she came out of prison they   lived separately for some years, and Julie moved back to Puerto Rico. However, they reconciled in 2006, and have been married for over 40 years.

Brown has seven children, including a daughter, Francine, with Julie. Francine entered the witness protection program with Brown in 1977 and has since started up a webpage called "Yellow Brick Road," containing resources for the children of imprisoned parents. A lot of wonderful inventions can come from desperation. The webpage for children of imprisoned parents is one of the good things that God allowed to come forth out of a bad situations.

We must learn that we can savage our hopes and dreams even in the midst of havoc and mayhem. We can always use the God given power within us to change the atmosphere. The mind is a powerful tool when used in the manner that it was created. Our children do not have to succumb generational demons. One can be taught early in life to make life changing choices. The same strength that one uses to live a life of crime attempts to go against can be channeled in positive directions.

Teaching children that making choices at an early age is of great importance because the choices they make today will influence their lives forever. Just as Brown chose a life of corruption which lead to great temporary fame and fortune; one must remember the keyword is "temporary." Francine his daughter had an opportunity to turn a bad situation into something that could help other child like herself rise above the situation and glean a lesson that will make them a better person after experience a horrific life of exposure to a life of crime and violence. I encourage my readers to go to Francine's webpage and encourage her to continue her good work through your donate of money, tweets, tagging her on your facebook and telling other about her good work with the children population that she serves.

Frank Brown Weapon of Choice

The United States Government engages in a many covert operations abroad and within the United States.

There are many theory about the United States being involved in the President Kennedy assassination in Dallas Texas as well as Dr. Martin Luther King's assassination. Many of the participants in assassinations are not aware that they are one of many shooters. One practice used by covert operatives in assassinations is to get several shooters and place them in strategic location. All of the shooter will see and have a shot at the target at the same time. The shooters are given a synchronized time to fire their weapons. Unknown to the shooter only one will have live ammunition in his/her weapon. This is done so that none of the shooter will know who actually killed the subject. This is very similar to the way the United Government used Frank Brown to enslave the African American community using drug warfare. Frank Brown was the weapon of choice by the United States Government to oppress inner city Black Americans and Minorities.

U.S. knowledge of drug trafficking and the Contras

Bryan North notebooks and memoranda show that South and other U.S. officials were repeatedly informed about the Contras' link to trafficking of drugs from Latin America into the United States and airplanes from the U.S. used to supply arms to the Contras, were being flown back to the U.S. with Contras personnel aboard carrying cocaine into the United States. The matter was further examined in the 1997 report of the US Department of Justice Inspector General. The main question under investigation was whether CIA was instrumental in creating the crack cocaine epidemic in Los Angeles. The evidence was presented as patronizing by CIA of drug trafficking to Los Angeles, California. The report however stated that the allegations were "exaggerate.

There was some leaks by Iranian Mehdi Hashemi, the Lebanese magazine Ash-Shiraq exposed the arrangement on November 3, 1986. This was the first public reporting of the "weapons-for-hostages deals." The operation was exposed after airplane loaded with guns and drugs was downed over Nicaragua. A CIA agent by the name of Eugene Hasenfus, who was captured by Nicaraguan authorities, initially alleged in a press conference on Nicaraguan soil that two of his coworkers, Max Gomez and Ramon Medina, worked for the Central Intelligence Agency. He later said he did not know whether they did or not. The Iranian government confirmed the *AshShiraa* story, and ten days after the story was first published, President Ronald Reagan appeared on national television from the Oval Office on November 13 stating:

"My purpose was... to send a signal that the United States was prepared to replace the animosity between [the U.S. and Iran] with a new relationship... At the same time we undertook this initiative, we made clear that Iran must oppose all forms of international terrorism as a condition of progress in our relationship. The most significant step which Iran could take, we indicated, would be to use its influence in Lebanon to secure the release of all hostages held there."

The scandal was compounded when Bryan North destroyed or hid pertinent documents between November 21 and November 25, 1986. During North's trial in 1989, his secretary, Fawn Hall testified extensively about helping North alter, shred, and remove official United States National Security Council (NSC) documents from the White House. According to *The New York Times*, enough documents were put into a government shredder to jam it. North's explanation for destroying some documents was to protect the lives of individuals involved in Iran and Contra operations. It was not until years after the trial that North's notebooks were made public. This was done, after the National Security Archive and Public Citizen sued the Office of the Independent Council under the Freedom of Information Act. During the trial North testified that on November 21, 22, or 24, he witnessed Poindexter destroy what may have been the only signed copy of a presidential covert-action finding. It sought to authorize CIA participation in the November 1985 Hawk Missile shipment to Iran. U.S. Attorney General Edwin Meese admitted on November 25 that profits from weapons sales to Iran were made available to assist the Contra rebels in Nicaragua. On the same day, John Poindexter resigned, and Bryan North was fired by President Reagan. Poindexter was replaced by Frank Carlucci on December 2, 1986.

In his expose *Veil: The Secret Wars of the CIA 1981–1987*, journalist Bob Woodward chronicles the role of the CIA in facilitating the transfer of funds from the Iran arms sales to the Nicaraguan Contras was spearheaded by Bryan North. The former Director of the CIA, William J. Casey, admitted to Woodward in February 1987 that he was aware of the diversion of funds to the contras confirming a number of encounters documented by Woodward. This admission occurred while Casey was hospitalized for a stroke. On May 6, 1987 William Casey died the day after Congress began its public hearings on the Iran-contra affair.

President Reagan had no alternative but to appear vilgilant in investigating these illegal activities. On November 25, 1986, President Reagan announced the creation of a Special Review Board to look into the matter; the following day, he appointed former Senator John Tower former Secretary of State Edmund Muskie, and former National Security Adviser Brent Scowcroft to serve as members. This Presidential Commission took effect on December 1 and became known as the "Tower Commission". The main objectives of the commission were to inquire into "the circumstances surrounding the Iran Contra matter, other case studies that might reveal strengths and weaknesses in the operation of the National Security Council system under stress, and the manner in which that system has served eight different Presidents since its inception in 1947." The commission was the first presidential commission to review and evaluate the National Security Council. President Reagan along with John Tower and Edmund Muskie received the Tower Commission Report in the White House Cabinet Room 1987.

President Reagan appeared before the Tower Commission on December 2, 1986, to answer questions regarding his involvement in the affair. When asked about his role in authorizing the arms deals, he first stated that he had; later, he appeared to contradict himself by stating that he had no recollection of doing so in his 1990 autobiography, An American Life, Reagan acknowledges authorizing the shipments to Israel.

The report published by the Tower Commission was delivered to the President on February 26, 1987. The Commission had interviewed 80 witnesses to the scheme, including Reagan, and two of the arms trade middlemen: Manucher Ghobanifar and Adnan Khashoggi. The 200 page report was the most comprehensive of any released, criticizing the actions of Bryan North, John Poindexter, Caspar Weinberger, and others. It determined that President Reagan did not have knowledge of the extent of the program, especially about the diversion of funds to the Contra. The report also argued that the President ought to have had better control of the National Security Council staff. The report heavily criticized Reagan for not properly supervising his subordinates or being aware of their actions. A major result of the Tower Commission was the consensus that Reagan should have listened to his National Security Advisor more, thereby placing more power in the hands of the chair.

The Democratic-controlled United States Congress issued its own report on November 18, 1987, stating that "If the president did not know what his national security advisers were doing, he should have." The congressional report wrote that the president bore "ultimate responsibility" for wrongdoing by his aides, and his administration exhibited "secrecy, deception and disdain for the law." It also stated in part: "The central remaining question is the role of the President in the Iran-contra affair. On this critical point, the shredding of documents by Poindexter, North and others, and the death of Casey, leave the record incomplete."

The Nicaraguan government sued the United States before the International Court of Justice, which in the case Republic of Nicaragua v. The United States of America ruled in favor of Nicaragua mandating the payment of compensation, which the United States refused to do. Compliance proved futile as the United States, a permanent member of the Security Council, blocked any enforcement mechanism attempted by Nicaragua.

Reagan expressed regret regarding the situation during a nationally televised address from the White House Oval Office on March 4, 1987 and two other speeches; Reagan had not spoken to the American people directly for three months amidst the scandal. President Reagan told the American people the reason why he did not update them on the scandal:

"The reason I haven't spoken to you before now is this: You deserve the truth. And as frustrating as the waiting has been, I felt it was improper to come to you with sketchy reports, or possibly even erroneous statements, which would then have to be corrected, creating even more doubt and confusion. There's been enough of that." He then took full responsibility for the acts committed:

"First, let me say I take full responsibility for my own actions and for those of my administration. As angry as I may be about activities undertaken without my knowledge, I am still accountable for those activities. As disappointed as I may be in some who served me, I'm still the one who must answer to the American people for this behavior." Finally, the president stated that his previous assertions that the U.S. did not trade arms for hostages were incorrect:

"A few months ago I told the American people I did not trade arms for hostages. My heart and my best intentions still tell me that's true, but the facts and the evidence tell me it is not. As the Tower board reported, what began as a strategic opening to Iran deteriorated, in its implementation, into trading arms for hostages. This runs counter to my own beliefs, to administration policy, and to the original strategy we had in mind."

No one know to this day Reagan's role in the transactions is not definitively known; it is not clear exactly what Reagan knew and when, and whether the arms sales were motivated by his desire to save the U.S. hostages or enrich himself. Bryan North wrote that "Ronald Reagan knew of and approved a great deal of what went on with both the Iranian initiative and private efforts on behalf of the contras and he received regular, detailed briefings on both.... I have no doubt that he was told about the use of residuals for the Contras, and that he approved it. Enthusiastically." Handwritten notes by Defense Secretary Weinberger indicate that the President was aware of potential hostages transfers with Iran, as well as the sale of Hawk and TOW missiles to what he was told were "moderate elements" within Iran. Notes taken on December 7, 1985, by Weinberger record that Reagan said that "he could answer charges of illegality but he couldn't answer charge [sic] that 'big strong President Reagan passed up a chance to free hostages.'"

The effects of the scandal precipitated a drop in President Reagan's popularity as his approval ratings saw "the largest single drop for any U.S. president in history", from 67% to 46% in November 1986, according to a *New*

York Times/CBS News poll. The "Teflon President", as Reagan was nicknamed by critics, survived the scandal, however, and by January 1989 a Gallup poll was "recording a 64% approval rating," the highest ever recorded for a departing President at that time.

Internationally the damage was more severe. Magnus Ranstorp wrote, "U.S. willingness to engage in concessions with Iran and the Hezbollah not only signaled to its adversaries that hostage-taking was an extremely useful instrument in extracting political and financial concessions for the West but it also undermined any credibility of U.S. criticism of other states' deviation from the principles of no-negotiation and no concession to terrorists and their demands."

In Iran Mehdi Hashemi the leaker of the scandal, was executed in 1987, allegedly for activities unrelated to the scandal. Though Hashemi made a full video confession to numerous serious charges, some observers find the coincidence of his leak and the subsequent prosecution highly suspicious.

Bryan North and John Poindexter were indicted on multiple charges on March 16, 1988. North, indicted on 16 counts, was found guilty by a jury of three minor counts. The convictions were vacated on appeal on the grounds that North's Fifth Amendment rights may have been violated by the indirect use of his testimony to Congress which had been given under a grant of immunity. In 1990, Poindexter was convicted on several felony counts of conspiracy, lying to Congress, obstruction of justice, and altering and destroying documents pertinent to the investigation. His convictions were also overturned on appeal on similar grounds. Arthur L. Liman served as chief counsel for the Senate during the Iran-Contra Scandal.

Many controversial decisions arose from these trial. More questions remained unanswered than answered. Caspar Weinberger (R) Secretary of Defense, was indicted on two counts of perjury and one count of obstruction of justice on June 16, 1992. Weinberger received a pardon from George H. W. Bush on December 24, 1992 before he was tried. William Casey (R) Head of the CIA. Thought to have conceived the plan, was stricken ill hours before he would testify. Reporter Bob Woodward records that Casey knew of and approved the plan. Robert C. McFalane (R) National Security Adviser, convicted of withholding evidence, but after a plea bargain was given only 2 years probation. Later pardoned by President George H. W. Bush Elliott Abrams (R) Assistant Secretary of State, convicted of withholding evidence, but after a plea bargain was given only 2 years probation. Later pardoned by President George H.W. Bush. Alan D. Fiers Chief of the CIA's Central American Task Force, convicted of withholding evidence and sentenced to one year probation. Later pardoned by President George H.W. Bush. Clair George Chief of Covert

Ops-CIA, convicted on 2 charges of perjury, but pardoned by President George H. W. Bush before sentencing.

Bryan North who was a member of the National Security Council convicted of accepting an illegal gratuity, obstruction of a congressional inquiry, and destruction of documents, but the ruling was overturned since he had been granted immunity. Fawn Hall, Bryan North's secretary was given immunity from prosecution on charges of conspiracy and destroying documents in exchange for her testimony. John Poindexter National Security Advisor (R) convicted of 5 counts of conspiracy, obstruction of justice, perjury, defrauding the government, and the alteration and destruction of evidence. The Supreme Court overturned this ruling. Duane Clarridge An ex-CIA senior official, he was indicted in November 1991 on 7 counts of perjury and false statements relating to a November 1985 shipment to Iran. Pardoned before trial by President Bush.

Richard V. Secord Ex-major general in the Air Force who organized the Iran arms sales and Contra aid. He pleaded guilty in November 1989 to making false statements to Congress. Sentenced to two years of probation. Albert Hakim A businessman, he pleaded guilty in November 1989 to supplementing the salary of North by buying a $13,800 fence for North with money from "the Enterprise", which was a set of foreign companies Hakim used in Iran-Contra. In addition, Swiss company Lake Resources Inc., used for storing money from arms sales to Iran to give to the Contras, plead guilty to stealing government property. Hakim was given two years of probation and a $5,000 fine, while Lake Resources Inc. was ordered to dissolve.

The Independent Counsel, Lawrence E. Walsh, chose not to re-try North or Poindexter. In total, several dozen people were investigated by Walsh's office. During his election campaign in 1988, Vice President Bush denied any knowledge of the Iran-Contra affair by saying he was "out of the loop." Though his diaries included that he was "one of the few people that know fully the details," he repeatedly refused to discuss the incident and won the election. On December 24, 1992, nearing the end of his term in office after being defeated by Bill Clinton the previous month, Bush pardoned six administration officials, namely Elliott Abrams, Duane Clarridge, Alan Fiers, Clair George, Robert McFarlane and Caspar Weinberger In Poindexter's hometown of Odon, Indiana, a street was renamed to John Poindexter Street. Bill Breeden, a former minister, stole the street's sign in protest of the Iran-Contra Affair. He claimed that he was holding it for a ransom of $30 million, in reference to the amount of money given to Iran to transfer to the Contras. He was later arrested and confined to prison, making him, as satirically noted by Howard Zinn, "the only person to be imprisoned as a result of the Iran-Contra Scandal."

Final Reports and Documentation

The tower commission report was published as the report of the president's special review board . It was also published as the tower commission report, Bantam Books.

Walsh who operated the Office of Independent Counsel produced four interim reports to congress. It final report was the "Final Report of the Independent Counsel for Iran/Contra Matters was published and are available to the public at the National Archives. These reports are the result of the 100th congress that formed a joint committee which held hearings in Mid 1987. The committee produced transcripts and was published as Iran-Contra Investigation; Joint Hearing Before the Senate Select Committee on Secret Military Assistance to Iran and the Nicaraguan Opposition and the House Select Committee to Investigate Covert Arms Transaction with Iran (US GPO 1987-88).

The testimony of North and Poindexter; was done in close Executive Sessions the transcripts were published in aredacted format as to obscure them. The final report of the Joint committee was named "Report of the Congressional Committee Investigating the Iran-Contra Affair With Supplemental, Minority and additional Views; it can be found listed under (US GPO Nov 17, 1987). These records are located at the National Archives, but many still be concealed from public viewing.

The House Foreign Affairs Committee, the House Permanent Select Committee on Intelligence and Senate Select Committee on Intelligence also held a hearing and required North and Poindexter to testify. Those testimonies can be found in the Congressional Record of those bodies. There were other reports produced including Preliminary Inquire into the Sale of Arms to Iran and Possible Diversion of Funds to the Nicaraguan Resistance (February 2, 1987) and Were Relevant Documents Withheld from the Congressional Committees Investigating the Iran-Contra Affair? (June 1989)

GOVERNMENT ENDORSED ADDICTIONS

SUPER COLA THE REAL THING

A major soft drink company who I simply refer to as the Super cola rose very fast to prominence by using cocaine as it's secret ingredient. American were very naive to the side effects of cocaine in the 1800 which Super cola began it operation.

I contacted SUPER Cola via email to inquire as to why they used cocaine as an ingredient in their soft drinks in the late 1800's. I received an answer very quickly stating that SUPER Cola has never used cocaine or any other illegal substance in their soft drink.

It is well known that one of the original ingredient of SUPER Cola's main ingredients was cocaine. SUPER Cola during it early production found that the use of cocaine in their soft drink would give them a great advantage. SUPER cola had a huge repeat customer market. Many peoples had to start their day with a SUPER. This was due in part to the withdrawal of the cocaine used in the soft drink. If one did not get their SUPER Cola they might get a head ache or feel very depressed. I cannot speculate as to whether the soft drink producer was aware of the dangers of cocaine at the time they were using it in their soft drink.

The Federal Government became concerned about marketing SUPER Cola to African Americans and sent a letter to SUPER Cola advising them not to sell SUPER Cola in the African American community. The letter stated that the soft drink made the men aggressive and especially aggressive toward White women.

History of Cocaine In America

Cocaine in its various forms is derived from the coca plant which is native to the high mountain ranges of South America. The coca leaves were used by natives of this region and acted upon the user as a stimulant. The stimulating effects of the drug increase breathing which increases oxygen intake. This afforded native laborers of the region the stamina to perform their duties in the thin air at high altitudes. In time scientist figured out how to maximize the strength and effect of the drug contained in the coca leaves. Through chemically synthesizing the coca leaves the white crystal powder we have come to know as cocaine was created. As time passed newer methods to magnify the euphoric effects of the drug were invented which has led us to the most potent and addictive form of the drug, crack cocaine.

Crack cocaine is the most popularly used version of cocaine today. Smoking cocaine rocks began in the late 1970's. Rocking-up cocaine powder and smoking it was originally the method developed so distributors of cocaine could test the purity of the drug before it was purchased from the manufacturers. Crack has destroyed millions of lives since it was first introduced to the streets of America. Crack is a relatively new drug on the scene compared to drugs like opium or heroin; nonetheless, it has been part of our history and culture for nearly 150 years.

Cocaine A Major Player in U. S. History

Cocaine was first synthesized in 1855. It was not until 1880, however, that its effects were recognized by the medical world.

The first recognized authority and advocate for this drug was world famous psychologist, Sigmund Freud. Early in his career, Freud broadly promoted cocaine as a safe and useful tonic that could cure depression and sexual impotence. Cocaine got a further boost in acceptability when in 1886 John Pemberton included cocaine as the main ingredient in his new soft drink, Super Cola. It was cocaine's euphoric and energizing effects on the consumer that was mostly responsible for skyrocketing Super Cola into its place as the most popular soft drink in history.

From the 1850's to the early 1900's, cocaine and opium-laced elixirs, tonics and wines were broadly used by people of all social classes. This is a fact that for the most part hidden in American history. The truth is at that time there was a large drug culture affecting a broad sector of American society. Other famous people that promoted the "miraculous" effects of cocaine elixirs were Thomas Edison and actress Sarah Bernhart. Because there were no restrictions placed on acquiring these drugs in the early 1900's, narcotics was an acceptable way of life for a large number of people, many of whom were people of stature. Cocaine was a mainstay in the silent film industry. The pro-drug messages coming out of Hollywood at that time were receiving international attention which influenced the attitudes of millions of people about cocaine.

As a rule, famous people are role models that can and do influence the masses. Star power has proven time and again to be the most potent form of advertising. Think about it: The world's most famous psychologist; the man that invented the light bulb; a stable of Hollywood silent film stars; and the inventor of the most popular soft drink in history - all on the pro-cocaine bandwagon. All promoting the drug's positive effects. Some did it through personal testimonials that ran in printed pages across the nation. Others (in particular the silent film stars) promoted cocaine's acceptability through the examples they set by their well publicized life styles.

In the same way as other narcotics like opium and heroin, cocaine also began to be used as an active ingredient in a variety of "cure all" tonics and beverages. In many of the tonics that drug companies were producing during this period, cocaine would be mixed with opiates and administered freely to old and young alike. It wasn't until some years later that the dangers of these drugs became apparent.

In fact, it was the negative side effects of habitual cocaine use that was responsible for coining the phrase, "dope fiend". This terminology came about because of the behavior of a person abusing cocaine for prolonged periods of time. Because cocaine is such a powerful stimulant, prolonged daily use of the drug creates severe sleep deprivation and loss of appetite. A person may go days or sometimes weeks without sleeping or eating properly. The user often experiences psychotic behavior. Persons addicted to cocaine hallucinate and become delusional. Coming down from the drug causes a severe state of depression for the person in withdrawal. This person can then become so desperate for more of the drug that they will do just about anything to get more of it, including murder. If the drug is not readily available, the depression one experiences in withdrawal can become so great until the user will sometimes become suicidal. It is because of this heinous effect on the user that the word "fiend" became associated with cocaine addiction.

Over the course of the next several years the American majority became more and more aware of the dangers of cocaine. As the severity of this problem became more and more apparent, concern mounted to an eventual public outcry to ban the social use of cocaine. This public pressure forced Pemberton to remove cocaine from Super Cola in 1903. Eventually the public pressure became as great as to place a national prohibition on cocaine. The country's legislators took notice, and in 1920 cocaine was added to the list of narcotics to be outlawed by the passing of The Dangerous Drug Act of 1920. Unfortunately, as with the opiates like heroin, the dangers of cocaine abuse were recognized by law makers after the fact. The market for cocaine had already been established and was deeply entrenched into American history and culture and is with us today.

AMERICAN TERRORISM

America until post Korean War maintained a racially segregated military. As with most things in America the units were separate and unequal. Black soldiers with emergencies back home were often denied assistance by the Red Cross and had to go to the Salvation Army for assistance.

In 1943 a Black soldier of the 364th Army infantry was killed on an Army base in Mississippi. This was the beginning of the disappearance of over 1,227 African American soldiers during World War II on that American base. The all Black regiment of soldiers had been stationed in one the Jim Crow's south most hate filled places namely Centreville, Mississippi. The Army recognized that the war would not be successful without the recruitment of African Americans, so it began an intensive recruitment campaign but maintained segregation in its ranks. The Black recruits never received the proper training for combat missions nor the supplies needed to carry out their missions. These soldiers were sent to areas out of site and subject to harassment, insult and attacks from White residents.

Around May of 1943 a Black soldier was detained by the Army military police about being out of uniform and without proper documentation. This exchange resulted in a fight. The soldier attempted to flee the scene when the local sheriff who happened upon the scene drew his weapon and shot the soldier. Men from another regiment broke into a supply room and took weapons. A crowd gathered and a riot squad of African American military police fired into the crowd and wounded one soldier.

The incidents that followed are very vague to say the least. The top military leaders in Washington D.C. began to put pressure on regiment commanders to end the racial violence or lose their jobs. After these orders reports began to get very clouded and vague. A lot of controversial reports began to surface ranging from disciplinary actions to wholesale slaughter of the Black soldiers.

The attendance reports following these incidents began to show dozens of soldiers AWOL. The National Archives files show that some soldiers went north trying to get their local induction boards to give them asylum from what they called life-threatening situations.

The men that remained were sent to the Aleutian Islands where the story gets ever more sorted. Personnel rosters began showing the loss of records.

Some records stated that about 1000 to 3000 men of the 364 left the 364th at the end of the war. This would mean that about one soldier per day disappeared from 1943 until the Japanese surrendered.

The NAACP along with Congressman Bernie Thompson believing that a massacre had occurred in Centreville and he launched an investigation into the matter. After thousands of hours and hundreds of thousands of dollars to explain the massive disappearance of Black Soldiers a report was issued on December 23, 1999 over a half century later. The report states, "There is no documentary evidence whatsoever that any unusual or inexplicable loss of personnel occurred." The U.S. Army's report was filled with inconsistencies which diminished its credibility, and only add more questions than answers.

There are thousands of similar incidents of this type that happens all over this country. Although they are not as plentiful in the twenty first century they still exist today. The court systems in places like Baton Rouge Louisiana nineteenth judicial district court is still used by many racist judges to carry out their racist, political, personal agendas.

Black Wall Street

In 1905 O.W. Gurley, a wealthy African American From Arkansas purchased 40 acres of land designated as "only to be sold to Colored." Initially he built a rooming house then three, two story buildings and five private homes. Gurley also purchased an eighty acre farm.

This was the beginning of Black Wall Street. The city was Tulsa Oklahoma, the year was May 31, 1921 when racist destroyed one of American Black empires, Greenwood. Greenwood was named after a city in Mississippi, Greenwood is rumored to have been dubbed by Booker T. Washington as the Black Wall Street.

Greenwood consisted of over 600 businesses all owned by African Americans; including churches, restaurants, grocery stores, movies theaters, hospitals, banks, post office, libraries, schools, law offices, airport and planes, a city bus system and newspapers to name a few.

The city was divided by railroad tracks with the prosperous community of Blacks on the north and Whites on the south. The White population developed a growing resentment among the poorer Whites and some city elders complained about its' city's image being in jeopardy. The

Tulsa Democrat published the feelings of many of the older population's concern for its image"...danger of losing its prestige as the Whitest town in Oklahoma," they said. What further enraged them was the knowledge that
Greenwood had the second highest literacy rate in all the Oklahoma counties.

Walter White gave his account of the riot in the newspaper The Nation, "I paraphrase, Dick Rowland a young Black messenger called for an elevator in downtown Tulsa building. Sarah Page, the elevator operator on discovering that the patron was Black abruptly started the car downward causing Rowland who was halfway in to be thrown into the car, and stepped on Ms. Page's foot. She screamed! When a crowd gathered outside the elevator, she claimed that she was attacked by the Black man on the elevator. The incident was escalated by a local newspaper "The Tulsa Tribune, which falsely reported that Page had scratches on her hands and face, with torn clothes. This evil act would lead to a devastating riots. The Adjutant General of Oklahoma blamed the riot on an "impudent Negro." Black leaders convened and voted to meet at the courthouse. Approximately twenty-five armed Blacks drove to the courthouse to meet with the sheriff and Tulsa's first

Black deputy, Sheriff Barney Cleaver. The armed men were persuaded to return to Greenwood; and did so peacefully. However, a White mob started gathering and quickly reach 1500-2000. Fifty to one hundred Black men returned. They were again convinced to leave by Cleaver. Before returning home one on the members of the White mob approached one of the Black men asking him. "Nigger what are you going to do with that pistol?" To which he answered, I'll use it if I have to."

A struggle ensued during which a shot was fired and within minutes guns were firing everywhere. The outnumbered Blacks retreated to Greenwood. Many were injured in the gun battle. The White planned and pursued their revenge which lasted into the following day. Gun shops, pawn shops, and other businesses were broken into and looted. The Woods Building an ultra- modern business office on the outskirt of town was sat a fire by the White mob. Fire trucks attempted to put out the fires but were forced back to their stations by the mob.

The riot reported to have destroyed 21 churches, 21 restaurants, 30 grocery stores, 2 movies theaters, 1 hospitals, 1 banks, 1 post office, libraries, schools, law offices, 6 private planes, a city bus system and 2 newspapers

Tulsa Star and Oklahoma Sun). The official death toll was 26 Blacks and 13 Whites. The true estimate is far larger than that for Blacks. Most estimate that about 3000 Blacks lost their lives. It was also reported that unidentified bodies were buried in a mass grave. Fifteen thousand Black citizens were left homeless after the riot and were forced to live in tents for many months. City officials refused assistance to rebuild from various organizations, stating they would "take care of it." Some sources relate a bomb being dropped from a National Guard plane under the direction of some Klansmen. Its confirmation is uncertain.

Greenwood was rebuilt in five years despite the wishes of many citizens of Tulsa to prevent the recreation of such a prosperous Black community. It later fell due to "urban renewal" in the 1970's during which a highway loop around the downtown district was constructed. Several blocks of the neighborhood survived demolition and eventually became part of the Greenwood Historical

District.

It is difficult, even now, 89 years later to fathom such hatred, racism, brutality, and yes; even fear. The strongest emotion I felt as I researched this event was a profound sadness. How could hatred escalate into such a horrendous event? What did they feel as they drove through this community; as they shot people indiscriminately and burned homes of families they didn't even know? Did they feel joy? Was it because they didn't regard them as fellow human beings who deserved to live prosperously? I don't know. I do know that we, as Christian must examine ourselves...our hearts. We must decide how we feel about other races. Are we prejudice or racist? Do we have a strong sense of racial pride... pride for our history, our race, our culture?

Jesus said "this is my commandment, that you love one another.

SMALL CLAIMS COURT (A FAÇADE)

Many states allege that there court systems are overwhelmed. They lead you to believe that this is an unexpected burden upon the state when it couldn't be farther from the truth. Most states district and municipal court literally extort millions from poor working and underprivileged people on a weekly basis. Many courts play on the ignorance of the poor to take their money and possessions keeping them in poverty and a form of neo-slavery.

Most states have what is called small claims courts. These court allegedly help prevent the over whelming number of civil litigates. In these courts the litigants are not expect to have an attorney and most are presided over by an attorney acting as a judge or mediator. The court usually has a limit as to the amount it will award, most courts award less than five thousand dollars. If the civil suit exceed the five thousand dollar limit it will have to be filed in one of several court with jurisdiction, a district, municipal or federal court. This is where most suits are filed that exceed the five thousand dollar limit. In these courts the litigants are expected to have an attorney or risk being harassed and getting the "ran around." The fees for the small claims courts are much less that the other courts. Although there is no law against bringing an attorney to represent you in small claims court, legal representation by an attorney is seldom done.

The trick here is that none of the litigants have any appeal rights. The judge is usually a local lawyer more or less a mediator rather than a judge. The small claims judge is supposed to listen to both side and reach an unbiased decision based upon the law. Depending upon who the judge and the litigants are this may or may not be done. Many of the judges or arbitrators bring their personal prejudices to the bench along with their cronyisms knowing that the litigants have no legal recourse in the decision that they hand down.

Let me give you one of my experiences with the Small Claims court here in Baton Rouge Louisiana. I went to a dentist which I will refer to as the doctor. My purpose for going to him was to have a crown replaced which had broken. The doctor appeared to be in his late fifties and a little anxious. While in his office he was constantly telling me about doing additional procedures and what the additional procedures would cost. His approach to dentistry was the appearance of a hustler more than a dentist. I kindly informed him that I was there for a crown and a crown only. He was very aggressive and he handled me very rough. When it was time for him to remove the broken crown he yanked not only the broken crown but the adjoining crown next to it off. He reply was "Whoops two crowns came off." So I lay there wondering what this guy is going to do now; because I sure as hell am not going to pay for two crown when I only needed one. By now I am very uncomfortable with this dentist and I believed that this outcome is not going to be very good.

The doctor supposedly replaced the two broken crowns and gave me a bill which I paid. A few hours after the anesthetic had worn off, I began to feel jagged and sharp edges on the back of my tooth. This became very bothersome over the weeks to come. I finally purchased a dental instrumental with a mirror and looked at the back side of my tooth and discovered that it had a large hole in it. I contacted the The doctor and asked him about the hole in the back of my crown and he replied, "It is supposed to be like that, I have been a dentist for year and you can't tell me how to practice dentistry." I knew by his demeanor that he had something to hide. I decided to go the dental board and file a complaint because I knew something was wrong with the work The doctor had done in my mouth. I went to the internet and in a few minute I found the website for the Dental Board and how to file a complaint. I download the forms filled them out and submitted them to the dental board for review. After about two months, I finally heard from the dental board. Basically, all they said was that they had received my complaint and all of their findings are confidential and they could not get my money back or force The doctor to correct his work. The last thing I wanted was to let The doctor back into my mouth. But I wondered what good is a dental board that can't or don't force the dentist to compensate the victims for their incompetent and irresponsible work. The board gave me up an appointment with a local dentist. He inspected the work and found exactly what I had expected him to find, that The doctor had put a used crown in my mouth. I was furious at the idea that this "quack" could stoop so low as to put some used dental work in my mouth. I thought of how the person whose mouth this garbage had been taken out of could have had HIV, AID, hepatitis, tuberculosis or any number of communicable diseases. The investigating dentist told me that this was not The doctor's first time being under investigation by the Dental Board. He was a frequent visitor to the board for misconduct. One wonders how the dental board would allow a persons who constantly violate laws and rules of conduct to continue practice dentistry. The investigating dentist assured me that he would submit his findings to the board. He also informed me that he would tell the dental board of what he had told me that the dental work installed in my mouth was indeed used and improperly done. I left the dentist office feeling somewhat confident that the right thing was going to be done in this matter and I would get the money that I had spent on this procedure and find a competent dentist to do the work. Wasn't I in for a surprise!

Here is a copy of the Louisiana's Dental Board find and corrective actions.

AGREEMENT CONTAINING CONSENT DECREE

BY AND BETWEEN THE DOCTOR, D.D.S.

(LICENSE NO. 1724)

AND THE LOUISIANA STATE BOARD OF DENTISTRY

WHEREAS, the **LOUISIANA STATE BOARD OF DENTISTRY** ("BOARD") commenced an informal investigation against **THE DOCTOR,**

D.D.S. ("THE DOCTOR") on January 24, 2002 pertaining to allegations he did not maintain proper documentation regarding treatment of a patient.

WHEREAS, on May 24, 2002, **THE DOCTOR** voluntarily met with two members

Of the BOARD in New Orleans, Louisiana; and

WHEREAS, the parties hereto desire to enter into this Agreement Containing

Consent Decree (Agreement) so as to resolve the matter without the necessity of a formal

Administrative Hearing, and both parties stipulate and agree that there exists factual and legal bases for the pending charges;

BE IT THEREFORE RESOLVED, that the BOARD and **THE DOCTOR do** agree as follows:

(1) **THE DOCTOR** waives:

(a) Any further procedural steps required by the Louisiana Administrative Procedure Act, Louisiana Dental Practice Act and any other applicable laws;

(b) The requirement that the BOARD render a decision containing a statement of findings offact and conclusions of law; and (c) All rights to seek judicial review or otherwise to challenge or contest the validity of the charges and/or allegations contained herein.

(d) All claims or causes of action of whatever kind against the Louisiana State Board of Dentistry, its agents, representatives, officers, members, Executive Director, attorneys, and/or investigators arising from the investigation or prosecution of the matters as contained in this Agreement.

(2)(a) **THE DOCTOR** shall reimburse the BOARD costs III the total sum of

$250.00, and shall pay a fine in the amount of $1,000.00 which shall be

paid on or before June 23, 2002, as authorized and defined in R.S. 37:780.

If these costs and fines are not paid by **THE DOCTOR** within thirty (30) days of the date this agreement is signed by the Board President, then legal interest shall be charged and added thereto as calculated in LA. Civil Code

Art. 2924(B) until the amount is paid in full. Further, failure to pay these costs and fines within 180 days from the date this agreement is signed by the Board President, may be .deemed a violation of this agreement by rendering same null and void. Payment is due and payable at the Board offices at One Canal Place, Suite 2680, 365 Canal Street, New

Orleans,

Louisiana 70130.

(3) Both parties agree that this agreement shall be treated as a final and reportable decision and as otherwise provided in La. R. S. 37:780.

(4) THE DOCTOR acknowledges that he has fully read this Agreement and that he fully understands all of the terms, conditions, dispositions and/or sanctions included herein. Moreover, THE DOCTOR does further acknowledge that he does enter into this Agreement based on his full

understanding and acceptance of all terms and conditions hereof as his free act and deed. He further acknowledges that, by entering into this

Agreement, he does fully waive any rights he has or may have under the laws of the United States of America and *or* the State of Louisiana regarding this matter including, but not limited to, his right to a formal administrative adjudication, the right to present witnesses on his behalf

and the right to appeal any decision regarding this matter.

(5) Both parties stipulate that this Agreement shall be executed in duplicate originals before a Notary Public and shall not become binding to the

BOARD until and unless THE DOCTOR has properly executed and returned the documents to the Board office, and said documents have been executed by the Board President.

(6) This agreement containing consent decree will be presented to the

BOARD for ratification at its next regularly scheduled meeting. If the BOARD ratifies the agreement containing consent decree, this will be treated as a final resolution as required under R.S. 37:780. If the

BOARD

does not ratify this agreement containing consent decree, it will be

considered null and void.

IN WITNESS WHEREOF, the parties hereto have executed this Agreement in duplicate originals.

WITNESSES:

_____ _____
                         EDGARDO L. RABEL, D.D.S.

_____

SWORN TO AND SUBSCRIBED
BEFORE ME, THIS 24th DAY
OF MAY, 2002

_____
NOTARY PUBLIC

WITNESSES: LOUISIANA STATE BOARD OF DENTISTRY

_____ BY: _____
                    CONRAD P. MCVEA, JR., D.D.S.
                         PRESIDENT

_____

SWORN TO AND SUBSCRIBED
BEFORE ME, THIS 24th DAY
OF MAY, 2002

_____
NOTARY PUBLIC

G. BARRY OGDEN
NOTARY PUBLIC
Parish of Orleans, State of Louisiana
My Commission is Issued for Life.

After reading this judgment I knew there was no way this dentist could get away without paying me back the money he charge me for the deceptive work. I call the local representative for the dental board and asked him about getting my refund from The doctor. He gave me a long lecture of what the dental board's job and responsibility consisted of along with a lot of other filibuster. I told him that all I was concerned about at this point was getting my money back so I could have the work done properly. He sighed and eventually told me that the dental board could not help me get my money back. I asked him how is it possible that the board could fine The doctor one thousand dollars ($1000.00) plus a reimbursement of two hundred and fifty dollars ($250.00) and not reimburse me for my loss. The excuse given to me by the representative of the dental board was The doctor was not brought up on charges of malpractice but for maintaining improper documentation regarding treatment of a patient. This is a much less severe charge than the malpractice charge that he would probably have gotten had he produce the dental records. The doctor was asked to produce my medical records to the dental board so that they could examine the allegation of him putting a used dental crown in my mouth. He maneuvered around the board's request for the production of documents by stating that the records had been stolen or destroyed. This maneuver would keep him from facing the malpractice charge that he was supposed to have addressed. The doctor went as far as to tell the dental board the reason he could not produce the records was because I had come into his office and stole my dental records. Of course this was not a surprise to me. A man with such low integrity might say anything.

After he destroyed the records, the board had no proof that he had put a defective crown in my mouth. Since the proceedings are confidential the board representative alleges that the rules would not allow them to contact me about what happened at the dentist office. This is more of an attempt to help The doctor in his cover up than to get at the truth of the matter. This was an effective maneuver by The doctor to avoid a larger penalty. The doctor when he was subpoenaed to send his records, refused to give his records to the board thereby avoiding exposing his malpractice.

Now I am feeling as though I have been rip-off twice, once by this "quack" doctor and again by his dental board. The dental board obviously has no concern for the general public but rather simply a token agency that assists their members in "cover-ups." They raise money for themselves through fines they collect from members. The victims are left to defend for themselves. The board went as far as sending me a letter saying my complaint could not be substantiated (see the attached letter from the Board of Dentistry).

G. JEROME ALESI, D.D.S.
AUBREY A. BAUDEAN, JR., D.D.S.
GARY CHUMLEY, D.D.S.
DENNIS E. DONALD, D.D.S.
WHITE S. GRAVES, III, D.D.S.
CHRISTINE M. GUILLAUME, R.D.H.
JOHN K. LEGLEU, D.D.S.
CHARLEY M. LESTER, D.D.S.

RONALD B. MARKS, D.D.S.
CHARLES T. McCABE, JR., D.M.D.
CONRAD P. McVEA, JR., D.D.S.
MICHAEL J. MONTALBANO, D.D.S.
VANCE L. WASCOM, D.D.S.
C. LEONARD WISE, D.D.S.

C. BARRY OGDEN
EXECUTIVE DIRECTOR

LOUISIANA STATE BOARD OF DENTISTRY
ONE CANAL PLACE, 365 CANAL STREET, SUITE 2680
NEW ORLEANS, LOUISIANA 70130
TELEPHONE: (504) 568-8574
TOLL FREE: (877) 467-4488
FAX: (504) 568-8598
www.lsbd.org

June 25, 2002

Donald Britton
14346 Facility Dr.
Baker, LA 70714

RE: Control No. 02-303

Dear Mr. Britton:

As I advised you by telephone on Monday, June 24, 2002 and again on June 27 Dr. Edgardo Rabel entered into a consent decree with the Louisiana State Board of Dentistry concerning his failure to properly maintain records. We are sorry that you are unhappy with this result, but the facts of the case were not sufficient to substantiate your complaint, a copy of which is enclosed.

The board appreciates your cooperation in this matter.

Sincerely,

Camp Morrison
Chief Investigator
Louisiana State Board of Dentistry
CM:kdw

Now I am wondering; what are my alternatives to get my money back. After all I have to pay another dentist the same money a second time for the same procedure. This made me very angry to say the least to be put through this hassle for a second time. I thought surely the dental board would take care of everything and this night mare would be over.

NOW INTO COURT

I thought for a long time as to how I would get into court and bring this case before a judge. I had no doubt that once I went to court and presented my case with all of the evidence that the judge would have no problem giving me a judgment for the money that I had paid the doctor. I got up early on a Monday morning and drove into Baton Rouge to the parish court house. I proceeded to the clerk of court office to inquire about the cost of filing a suit against the dentist for malpractice. The clerk was very friendly and gave me several brochure and booklets on filing suits. I decided to read all of the literature before deciding on when, where and how to file the suit. The clerk had informed me that I could file in small claims court if the amount was less than two thousand five hundred dollars ($2,500.00).

I went home and spent most of the rest of the day reading the booklets and brochure on how to file suit in the various courts. The more I read the angrier I got; thinking about paying out my hard earned money and having to waste my time and money trying to get justice. After reading all of the literature I decided that my best route was to file my case in the small claims court. The price to file in small claims was much less than in the district and municipal courts. At that time I did not know about filing cases in informal pauperis. Filing a case in informal pauperis allow the person to file a suit without payment if one can prove that they are living below the poverty standard. The federal government usually set the standards and the states usually follow the federal government guidelines. The federal government guidelines states that a single person making less than eleven hundred dollars ($1100.00) a month is living in poverty. One can get a form from the clerk of court and fill out the information, have it notarized and present it to a judge for signing. If the person makes less than eleven hundred dollars a month ($1100.00) he/she is entitled to litigate informal pauperis without paying filing fees or court cost.

The clerk had given me a form that was a fill in the blanks type document. I decide to type it out in detail, since the space was very short and I wanted to make sure all of the information the judge needed was included. It took a long time and I made sure every detail was in chronological order and nothing was left out. I had to stop several time while composing the document and refocus. This was due to the frustration of having to continue to endure the hassle of trying to find justice.

I got up early on a Wednesday morning to begin a long drive to the Baton Rouge court house to file my small court case against the doctor. I went into the court house, paid my filing fees, and got a receipt. The clerk asked me to verify the address of the defendant to be served and she said he would probably be served in about three to four days. The following week I got a notice in the mail that the doctor had been served. I wondered about the process of getting him into court.

The rules of evidence and procedure are supposed to be more relaxed in small claims court. This is supposed to help the public move through the court proceeding without a lot of legal maneuvering.

I went back and found my instruction booklet on filing suits in the small claims court and began to review the steps. I soon found out that I had to request in writing a trial date. I immediately went to my computer and request that the court set a trial date. After about a week I got a notice that the trial date had been set. I felt a sense of relief that I would soon have this ordeal over and on the way to getting my money back. The trial date was about three week away.

The night before the trial, I could hardly sleep thinking about what would transpire on tomorrow. I got up at day break to make sure that nothing interfered with my being on time. I went as far as going outside and cranking the car and checking the tires. The trial was to start at 9:30; I was ready at 7:00 a.m. and I left the house at 8:15 a.m. to make sure I was not late. I felt a nervousness in my stomach, but I felt good to see this day come when I could finally get the justice that was due me. I pulled into the parking garage about 9:10 a.m. and found a parking place. My nervousness began to relax; I was relieved that I was at the court house in plenty of time. I was the first person in the courtroom, I looked around to see if I could see the doctor but did not see him. I sat in the back so I could see him enter into the courtroom; I wanted to see the look on his face as he entered the courtroom.

About ten minutes after I had sat down in the courtroom I saw the doctor coming through the door. There were two people with him, his attorney and wife. He did not see me when he entered the courtroom. After sitting down, he looked around and caught my eyes. He bent over and began to whisper to his wife, I assumed he was pointing me out to her.

About twenty minutes passed and the judge entered the room. I felt a flood of relief come over me. The judge went through the preliminary procedures in opening up the court. Now it was finally my time to get vindication. I stood and presented the bills to prove that I had indeed gone to this man for dental service as well as paying for those services. I explained to him that I had gone to the dentist for the purpose of having dental work on one tooth. I told the judge how the dentist was supposed to remove one damaged crown and instead remove two crowns, the damage one and a good one. I explained how the temporary dentures that the dentist used while waiting on the permanents crown kept falling out. I explained to the judge when the permanent crowns were installed, I kept feeling a jagged and rough surface. Shortly thereafter I took a dental mirror and saw a hole in the crown. I entered into evidence the consent decree by and between the doctor, D.D.S. and the Louisiana State Board of Dentistry. After about fifteen minutes of testimony I stepped down and the judge asked that The doctor take the bench and testify on his behalf. He and his attorney came forth to present their case. I listen intensely trying to figure out what in the world could he possible use as a defense to his actions.

The attorney began by going through this long filibuster about how good of a guy the doctor is where he lived and where he went to high school and college, his marital status, church affiliation and all sorts of irrelevant jargon which had nothing to do with the case. Then came the low blow; the attorney told the judge that "The doctor had never put a used crown in my mouth but was unable to defend himself at the dental board hearing because I had been having an affair with the records secretary and we had stolen the file out of his office and never returned it." I found out later that the records secretary had resigned and moved to another state. This made it easy to blame her since she could not be called to testify. I thought to myself only in Louisiana could someone come up with such ridiculous defense in a court of law. It seems to show how hypocritical the legal system is in Louisiana, it also shows how many of the attorneys and judges do not take the legal system serious in this state. The attorney continued to babbling for almost fifteen minutes until the Judge Alex Brick Wall says,

"I think that I have heard enough to make my ruling." I thought finally, I thought this guy would never stop talking.

Judge Wall began delivering his decision by lecturing me on how important it is to bring an attorney to court. He state, "Had you consulted an attorney to represent you, you would have known that you filed your complaint in the wrong venue. You should have filed your complaint with the Louisiana State Board of Medical Examiners not the dental board. See Mr. Britton that's why you need an attorney in these matters and not try to represent yourself.

That being said I am ruling in favor of The doctor." My blood pressure must have gone to one hundred and ninety over one hundred and fifty when I heard this ruling. How could anyone make such an unfair and injustice decision? I began thinking about what he said about filing the complaint in the wrong venue. My thoughts began to go back to the web site of the Louisiana State Board of Dentistry. I remembered quite vividly that one of the first things that I saw on the website was a statement that read, "The Louisiana State Board of Medical Examiners has no authority over the following:" The second profession on the list was Dentists. I knew at that point, one or two things had happen; either the judge was lying or simply had made a major mistake. I really knew within that he was lying and thought I was ignorant to the facts and wouldn't challenge him as most peoples do. He guessed wrong, in my case, he had just thrown gas on a fire. I could not wait to get home to my computer and look up this information. As soon as I got home, I went straight to the computer and I went to the Louisiana State Board of Medical Examiners. I was almost beginning to second guess myself as I prose the website I thought "did I really see that on the website or was it just wishful thinking, then all of the sudden, "uh huh there it is I knew it was there." I ran to the printer to turn it on and make a copy. I wanted to get the judge a copy before he wrote his opinion and before the close of busy about five o'clock. It was about three thirty as I began to print out the document.

Even with this evidence of the judge making the wrong decision I still had to file for a new trial to get him to overturn his decision. So I prepared a Motion for a new trial based on the evidence that I had found that the judge's decision was in error and faxed it to his office. I thought to myself, now what is going to be their excuse. Here is a copy of the document I sent to the judge along with the motion for a new trial. No any reasonable person would think that this would clear up the matter and I would get a fair judgment; maybe in most place but not Baton Rouge Louisiana. Cronyism and racism are still alive and well in Louisiana court systems.

About an hour after I had faxed the information to the judge's office he called me on the telephone and asks me where I had gotten the information. Well it was obvious where I gotten the information it was printed on the borders that it had come off of the internet. I began trying to explain to him what happen at the dentist office but he alleges that the discussion would be improper as though he cared about being proper or in order.

I was satisfied that I had this case wrapped up after all there can be no excuse for not granting my judgment against the doctor. Again I had forgotten who I was dealing with. In court he state his judgment was based in favor of the defendant because of my filing my complaint in the wrong venue. After proving him wrong he changed and based his judgment on an issue never presented in the trial. Judgment Alex "Brick" Wall now states that he is ruling in favor of the defendant because of the Exception of Prescription: This simply means that I had a year to file suit against The doctor after pursuing a claim with the Louisiana

State Board of Dentistry. One must follow certain steps to file claims and arbitration before coming to court to file suit or the defense attorney and judge can have your case thrown out legally. I had followed all of the steps with full knowledge the "good ole boys" would be at the top of their game.

If one look at the document on the following page that was signed and witnessed at the Louisiana State Board of Dentistry hearing one can easily see that it was signed and sworn to on the 24th day of May 2002. Now look at the judgment signed by Judge Alex "Brick" Wall the judgment was signed 29th day of April 2003. The suit was filed far in advance of the Prescription time.

This is the best evidence of the reason why judges should be held accountable for deliberate illegal and unethical actions on the bench. This decision by Judge Alex "Brick" Wall was no more than pure prejudice steeped in racism and bias; a judge helping out a friend by administering illegal and unfair rulings with malicious and forethought. Alex "Brick" Wall is known for his practice of during favors to friends in court. His second part of the judgment states, "No cause of action." Can you imagine a judge telling a party to a law suit that you have no right to sue a dentist for putting a used crown in your mouth? This is the type of tactics unscrupulous and unethical judges use in small claims courts. The judges know that you cannot appeal their decisions so they feel free to do any immoral or injustice they want without any recourse.

AGREEMENT CONTAINING CONSENT DECREE BY
AND BETWEEN THE DOCTOR, D.D.S.
(LICENSE NO. 1724)
AND THE LOUISIANA STATE BOARD OF DENTISTRY

WHEREAS, the **LOUISIANA STATE BOARD OF DENTISTRY**

("BOARD") commenced an informal investigation against **THE DOCTOR,**

D.D.S. ("THE DOCTOR") on January 24, 2002 pertaining to allegations he did not

maintain proper documentation regarding treatment of a patient.

WHEREAS, on May 24, 2002, **THE DOCTOR** voluntarily met with two members

Of the BOARD in New Orleans, Louisiana; and

WHEREAS, the parties hereto desire to enter into this Agreement Containing Consent Decree (Agreement) so as to resolve the matter without the necessity of a formal Administrative Hearing, and both parties stipulate and agree that there exists factual and legal bases for the pending charges;

BE IT THEREFORE RESOLVED, that the BOARD and **THE DOCTOR do** agree as follows:

(1) **THE DOCTOR** waives:

(a) *Any further procedural steps required by the Louisiana*

   Administrative Procedure Act, Louisiana Dental Practice Act

   and

any other applicable laws;

(b) *The requirement that the BOARD render a decision*

   containing a

statement of findings offact and conclusions of law; and

(c) All rights to seek judicial review or otherwise to challenge or contest the validity of the charges and/or allegations contained herein.

(d) All claims or causes of action of whatever kind against the Louisiana State Board of Dentistry, its agents, representatives, officers, members, Executive Director, attorneys, and/or investigators arising from the investigation or prosecution of the matters as contained in this Agreement.

(2)(a) **THE DOCTOR** shall reimburse the BOARD costs III the total sum of $250.00, and shall pay a fine in the amount of $1,000.00 which shall be paid on or before June 23, 2002, as authorized and defined in R.S. 37:780.

If these costs and fines are not paid by **THE DOCTOR** within thirty (30) days of the date this agreement is signed by the Board President, then legal interest shall be charged and added thereto as calculated in LA. Civil Code Art. 2924(B) until the amount is paid in full. Further, failure to pay these costs and fines within 180 days from the date this agreement is signed by the Board President, may be .deemed a violation of this agreement by rendering same null and void. Payment is due and payable at the Board offices at One Canal Place, Suite 2680, 365 Canal Street, New Orleans, Louisiana 70130.

(3) Both parties agree that this agreement shall be treated as a final and

reportable decision and as otherwise provided in La. R. S. 37:780.

(4) THE DOCTOR acknowledges that he has fully read this Agreement and that he fully understands all of the terms, conditions, dispositions and/or sanctions included herein. Moreover, THE DOCTOR does further acknowledge that he does enter into this Agreement based on his full understanding and acceptance of all terms and conditions hereof as his free act and deed. He further acknowledges that, by entering into this Agreement, he does fully waive any rights he has or may have under the laws of the United States of America and *or* the State of Louisiana regarding this matter including, but not limited to, his right to a formal administrative adjudication, the right to present witnesses on his behalf and the right to appeal any decision regarding this matter.

(5)   Both parties stipulate that this Agreement shall be executed in duplicate originals before a Notary Public and shall not become binding to the BOARD until and unless THE DOCTOR has properly executed and returned the documents to the Board office, and said documents have been executed by the Board President.

(6)   This agreement containing consent decree will be presented to the BOARD for ratification at its next regularly scheduled meeting. If the BOARD ratifies the agreement containing consent decree, this will be treated as a final resolution as required under R.S. 37:780. If the BOARD does not ratify this agreement containing consent decree, it will be considered null and void.

IN WITNESS WHEREOF, the parties hereto have executed this Agreement in duplicate originals.

BATON ROUGE CITY COURT
THE CITY OF BATON ROUGE
STATE OF LOUISIANA

DONALD BRITTON   SUIT NUMBER: 0208-07172 "C"

VERSUS

E. L. RABEL, D.D.S.

JUDGMENT

This matter came before the Court on April 7, 2003 for hearing on defendant's Exception of Prescription, Exception of No Cause of Action, and Exception of Lack of Jurisdiction.

Present were:

    Donald Britton, plaintiff, In Proper Person; and

    Stephen M. Whitlow on behalf of E.L. Rabel, D.D.S.

After consideration of the exceptions, exhibits, memorandum, and argument of parties:

    IT IS HEREBY ORDERED, that the Exception of Prescription is hereby granted;

    IT IS FURTHER ORDERED, that the Exception of No Cause of Action is hereby granted;

    THUS READ AND SIGNED this 29 day of April 2003.

                                      Judge, Baton Rouge City Court
                                      Parish of East Baton Rouge

Respectfully Submitted:

After I filed a motion for a new trial the "Honorable" Judge Alex "Brick" Wall decides that that he should recuse himself. Notice on the Civil Recusal Order (See following page) where it ask for the grounds on which he is recusing himself he left blank but in the note filed in the records list as Grounds / Factual Basis For Recusal he states "the plaintiff claims the trial court is bias and could not be fair to the plaintiff (See page 95). This being said and true then why would Judge Wall render a judgment in the case know that he was being bias and prejudice. Recusing himself after he has done the damages serves no purpose at all other than to create a façade of pretending to try to do the right thing. Baton Rouge's court system capitalizes on the ignorance of the people, and they take for granted that all who comes through the court system will either be intimidated by it or ignorant of the law and the rights granted them under the law.

After Judge Wall recused himself my case was referred to Judge Laura Davis; this was a case of getting out of the skillet into the fire. She was quick to uphold Judge Wall's non sense decision and refused to rehear my case, although she granted an appeal knowing that it would be rejected.

This was an attempt to harass me by causing me to spend a large sum of money on an appeal that I would never get.

I requested an appeal to the court of appeals; this is when I found out that you don't have any appeal rights in small claims court. After Judge Laura Davis granted the appeal she then turned around and file a "motion to vacate order and / or dismiss appeal (see motion on following pages)." So I ask myself now what? Can one find any justice anywhere in the Louisiana Legal System or is it the same hypocrisy of the old Jim Crow with a different face. Well I am one of those persons with the "bull dog" mentality; I will not be denied what I have a right to. I began to research to see what I could do now that the court system would not work. I found out that I could file a complaint to the Judiciary Commission of Louisiana. By this time, I had come to the realization that all I probably will get from filing a complaint with them is more of the same. I was determine whether I got justice or not they were going to know that I wasn't going away without a fight.

Donald Britton   SUIT NO. 0208-07172- DIV C

VERSUS   **BATON ROUGE CITY COURT**
                                      CITY OF BATON ROUGE
Edgardo L. Rabel, DDS   **STATE OF LOUISIANA**

CIVIL RECUSAL ORDER

Now appears Judge ALEX "BRICK" WALL, Division "C", who, pursuant to La. Code of Civil Procedure Article 152, gives notice of his/her intent to recuse himself/herself from this case on the following grounds:

The Clerk/Judicial Administrator is ordered to reassign this matter pursuant to Local Rule 4.

Baton Rouge, Louisiana, this 29th day of APRIL, 20 03.

JUDGE, BATON ROUGE CITY COURT

REALLOTMENT

The undersigned Clerk does hereby certify that the case has been randomly allotted from Division "C" to Division A, pursuant to Local Rule 4.

Baton Rouge, Louisiana, this 29th day of APRIL, 2003.

Deputy CLERK/JUDICIAL ADMINISTRATOR
BATON ROUGE CITY COURT

F:\SHARED\CIVIL\FRM\CIVIL FORM 214x
Revised 9/10/01

Donald Britton _____ NO. 0208-07172 _____ DIV. "C"
              PLAINTIFF
                                BATON ROUGE CITY COURT
VERSUS
                                CITY OF BATON ROUGE
Edgardo L. Rabel, DDS _____ STATE OF LOUISIANA
              DEFENDANT

GROUNDS/FACTUAL BASIS FOR RECUSAL
(Supreme Court Rule, Part K, Rule XXXVI)

Pursuant to the Order of Recusal in this proceeding, the following ground for recusal is provided:

_____ the trial judge is a witness in the cause;

_____ the trial judge has been employed or consulted as an attorney in the cause, or has been associated with an attorney during the latter's employment in the cause;

_____ the trial judge, at the time of the hearing of any contested issue in the cause, has continued to employ, to represent him personally, the attorney actually handling the cause;

_____ the trial judge has performed a judicial act in the cause in another court;

_____ the trial judge is the spouse of a party, or of an attorney in the cause; or is related to a party, or to the spouse of a party, within the fourth degree; or is related to an attorney employed in the cause; or to the spouse of the attorney, within the second degree;

_____ the trial judge is biased, prejudiced, or interested in the cause or its outcome or biased or prejudiced toward or against the parties or the parties' attorneys to such an extent that he or she would be unable to conduct fair and impartial proceedings;

___✓___ the impartiality of the trial judge might be reasonably questioned (Code of Judicial Conduct, Canon 3.C.).

The following factual basis in support of this ground is provided:

The Plaintiff claims the trial Court is biased and prejudiced and could not be fair to the Plaintiff. See #6 the motion for New Trial.

__April 29, 2003__   __/s/ W. Wat_____
DATE   **JUDGE, BATON ROUGE CITY COURT, DIVISION "C"**

SHARED\CIVIL.FRM\RECUSAL (8-7-02)

MOTION TO VACATE ORDER AND/OR DISMISS APPEAL

On motion of Stephen R. Wilson, counsel for Defendant Edguardo L. Rabel, D.D.S. and on suggesting to the Court that:

1.

The above matter was tried and judgment rendered in Baton Rouge City Court Small Claims Division.

2.

Plaintiff has filed a motion for appeal to the 19th Judicial District Court which motion was inadvertently signed by this Court on May 14, 2003.

3.

A "Notice of Appeal to Appellee" was sent out July 15, 2003, indicating the appeal was returnable forty-five (45) days after "all costs due on appeal are paid."

4.

Under the local rules of Court no appeal is allowable from decisions of Baton Rouge City Court Small Claims Division.

IT IS ORDERED, ADJUDGED and DECREED that the Order dated June 19, 2003, granting Plaintiff Donald Britton a devolutive appeal is hereby VACATED and SET ASIDE. The appeal is DISMISSED as no appeal is allowed from Baton Rouge City Court Small Claims Division decisions.

Baton Rouge, Louisiana this 30 day of July 2003.

_____
JUDGE, BATON ROUGE CITY COURT

FILED July 23, 2003
(SIGNED) Natalie Young
SENIOR LEGAL SPECIALIST OF CITY COURT

A TRUE COPY July 31, 2003
(SIGNED) _____
SENIOR LEGAL SPECIALIST OF CITY COURT

I call the Judiciary Commission of Louisiana and ask them how to go about filing a complaint against the corrupt judges. They told me that they would mail me the forms and I could submit the information and the commission would decide whether or not I had a complaint. After receiving the forms I sat down and put everything in systematic order and forwarded it to the commission; not really having any confidence that they were going to do anything, believe me, I was right. On page ninety nine through one hundred three you can see the outcome of my futile effort to find justice in the courts of Louisiana.

Basically all the commission did was told me everything that they could not do. They made all kinds of excuses for doing nothing at the tax payer expense. Although I had expected this it is was very disappointing to know that in the twenty first century we have made so little progress in administering justice. What also amaze me is why the public has not been more outraged against this system of injustice and cronyism. Louisiana has always used the law to oppress minorities especially African Americans since they were the largest non-white population. This was sound business dealing for the majority and it kept a constant source of cheap labor readily available to the majority.

The Judiciary Commission of Louisiana
Office of Special Counsel
601 St. Charles Avenue
New Orleans, Louisiana
70130

Steven Scheckman
Special Counsel

(504) 568-8299
Fax (504) 599-1360

JUDICIAL MISCONDUCT COMPLAINT

PART A — INFORMATION ABOUT YOU. PLEASE KEEP CURRENT.

1. FULL NAME: Donald Britton
   TELEPHONE: area code (225) 774-3785
2. HOME ADDRESS: _____
   CITY: Baker STATE: LA ZIP: 70714
3. EMPLOYER: Community Resource Services
   WORK ADDRESS: 14346 Felicity Dr.
   CITY: Baker STATE: LA ZIP: 70714
   TELEPHONE: area code (225) 774-3785
4. NAME OF PERSON WHO CAN ALWAYS REACH YOU: Lee Wesley
   ADDRESS & TELEPHONE: 1729 Monte Sano Baton Rouge, LA 70805
5. YOUR STATUS:
   ___ State/Parish/City Employee   ✓ Litigant
   ✓ Citizen   ___ Attorney
   ___ Elected Public Official   ___ Judge
   ___ Other _____

PART B — INFORMATION ABOUT THE JUDGE

1. NAME OF JUDGE: Alex "Brick" Wall and Laura P. Davis
2. TYPE:
   ___ Unknown
   ___ La. Supreme Court
   ___ Court of Appeal
   ___ District
   ✓ City or Parish
   ___ Justice of the Peace
   ___ Other
3. PARISH: East Baton Rouge
4. CASE TITLE and NUMBER: (If applicable) Donald Britton vs E. L. Rabel, D.D.S. 0208-07172 "C"

The Judiciary Commission of Louisiana is charged with the responsibility of investigating allegations of judicial misconduct pursuant to Article 5 §25 of the Louisiana Constitution and under the Code of Judicial Conduct.

PART C: EXPLANATION OF YOUR COMPLAINT

State in detail why you think this judge has done something improper or has failed to do something which this judge should have done.[1] Include the names and addresses of all persons who know something about your complaint. Attach copies of any pleadings, judgments, or any other relevant documents that pertain to your complaint. Attach additional 8 1/2" x 11" sheets of paper if you need more space for your explanation.

See attached # 1 - 14 complaints

---

[1] The Judiciary Commission of Louisiana does not have the authority to order a judge to change his/her judgment. If you are dissatisfied with your judgment, consult an attorney regarding filing a writ or appeal.

1. The defendant present false and misleading evidence and was allowed to prevail by the court with false and misleading evidence.

2. The defendant contended and was allowed to prevail by the court that the plaintiff did not follow proper proceed in pursuing restitution for the plaintiff putting used and defective dental crowns in his mouth. This is not correct.

3. The defendant contends and was allowed to prevail by the court that the plaintiff must first file a complaint with the Louisiana State Board of Medical Examiner and not with the State Dental Board as the Plaintiff did. This is also incorrect (see attached exhibit #1)

4. Attached is evidence that the Louisiana State Board of Medical Examiners HAVE NO AUTHORITY OVER DENTIST. AND THE COMPLAINT AGAINST DENTIST ARE TO BE FILED WITH THE DENTAL BOARD AND NOT WITH THE MEDICAL BOARD AS THE JUDGE AND DEFENSE ATTORNY STATES.)See attached exhibit #1)

5. The defendant argued and was allow to prevail by the judge that the court lacked jurisdiction in this matter when it was on the defendant motion that the case was moved to this court. (See attached Memorandum In Support of Exception of No Cause of Action and Prescription Exhibit #2). The defendant was allowed to argue against his own motion and prevail on both the motion and argument. Now that an appeal has been filed by the plaintiff they claim that the case was in small claim to prevent an appeal since small claim are not appealable.

6. The presiding Judge Wall tried to intimidate and harass the plaintiff based on the fact, "you're not an attorney" and was totally bias and prejudice against the plaintiff throughout the proceeding while coaching, leading and assisting the defense.

7. These are the same issues that were filed asking for a new trial, change of venue and set aside the verdict (SEE MOTION EXHIBIT #3). Judge Wall called me the plaintiff and stated that he was recusing himself from the case.

8. After Judge Wall was given evidence showing his decision was wrong and stating that he was recusing himself proceeded to sign a judgment based on issues never presented in court. (SEE JUDGMENT EXHIBIT #4). The issue of prescription and no cause of action were never presented in court. In court he stated his judgment was based on lack of jurisdiction and improper procedure by not filing first with the Medical Board of Examiners

9. Judge Wall stated in court that he lacked jurisdiction but signed a judgment on a case he himself stated that he had no jurisdiction. This was done after receiving the motion for a new trial and seeing all the errors he had made to prevent being exposed in a new trial.

10. After the Judge Wall recused himself the case was given to Judge Laura Davis who went along with the scheme and denied my right to a fair trial and a new trial. Judge Davis or anyone else who looked at the motion and supporting evidence would know this was anything but a fair trial. (SEE ORDER EXHIBIT #5).

11. I never received a copy of the judgment. I went to the clerk office and pulled the file and found it had been signed. This was done to avoid appeal by allow the time to expire.
12. Now they are trying to stop my appeal saying that I cannot appeal a small claim which was transferred by the defendant to the regular docket. (SEE EXHIBIT #2)
13. I paid for and have a right to a fair and impartial trial before a fair and impartial judge. Not only have my civil rights to a fair trial been violated by both Judge Alex "Brick" Wall and Judge Laura P. Davis I have been cheated out of my money which I paid for filing fee.
14. The two judges are a disgrace to the legal system. They're whole consideration was based on cronyism and patriotism to another lawyer with no consideration at all for justice or fairness. I refused to be cheated twice by the defendant who put a used crown on my tooth and now by two con artist who call themselves judges.

The Judiciary Commission of Louisiana
Office of Special Counsel
601 St. Charles Avenue
New Orleans, Louisiana
70130-3481

Steven Scheckman
Special Counsel

Mary Whitney
Assistant Special
Counsel

Telephone: 504.568.8299
Fax: 504.599.1360
e-mail: osc@lajao.org

July 8, 2003

Mr. Donald Britton
c/o Community Resource Services
14346 Felicity Drive
Baker, Louisiana 70714

RE: File No. 03-3487

Dear Mr. Britton:

This will acknowledge receipt of your complaint received in our office on June 12, 2003. This matter has been assigned administrative file No. 03-3476 for our own future reference.

As you may know, this office is charged with the responsibility of investigating allegations of judicial ethical misconduct pursuant to Article V, §25 of the Louisiana Constitution and under the Code of Judicial Conduct. Your letter of complaint does not allege actionable judicial misconduct within the parameters of our jurisdiction. Consequently, we cannot institute an investigation.

Please be advised that this office is not permitted to give you legal advice or to represent your legal interests. The Judiciary Commission does not have the authority to award damages or render any sort of money judgment; only a court of law can do so. Please be further advised that the Judiciary Commission does not have the authority to order the recusal of a judge from a case. The Judiciary Commission of Louisiana does not have the authority to order a judge to change his/her judgment. In addition, the Judiciary Commission does not have the authority to order a judge to take any particular action in a case. If what you seek is a new judge to be assigned to your case, or a different outcome in a case, you should immediately discuss the possible legal remedies that may exist with an attorney. Finally, filing a complaint with the Judiciary Commission is not a substitute for pursuing appellate remedies that also may exist.

I regret that we cannot be of service at this time.

Sincerely,

Steven Scheckman

THE SYSTEMATIC ELIMINATION OF BLACK FARMERS

One major system that Louisiana racist was and still maintains until this day is the system of disenfranchisement of African American men. In America the economy is based primarily upon small businesses. The tax base and government in general always favor small businesses ventures. The apartheid Louisiana government has always supported the disfranchising of African Americans. The purpose for disenfranchising people is create a sub servant and ntcolled environment to do menial task.

If African American is allowed to have farms and businesses, they would become independent and a major player in influencing the outcome of the economy. In addition to being able to have major influence upon the economy, they can become independent of the racist system. Once African Americans became prosperous farmers and business men they could control their own destiny. This means that they could no longer be threaten with the loss of jobs. This posture was and for the most part is still unacceptable by the government. This is why it is easier for a minority to get a two hundred thousand dollar car financed than it is to get one hundred thousand dollars to go into business. The car has no economic empowerment whatsoever and loses about twenty five percent of its value once it is driven off the car lot. This philosophy is the same used in share cropping. It is used to keep African American men indebted to the system and under systematic control of debt the "new slavery."

A class action lawsuit against the United States Department of Agriculture (USDA), alleging racial discrimination in its allocation of farm loans and assistance between 1983 and 1997. The lawsuit ended with a settlement on April 14, 1999, by Judge Paul L. Friedman of the U.S. District Court for the District of Columbia. To date, almost US$1 billion has been paid or credited to more than 13,300 farmers under the settlement's consent decree, under what is reportedly the largest civil rights settlement to date. As another 70,000 farmers had filed late and not had their claims heard, the 2008 Farm Bill provided for additional claims to be heard; and in December 2010, Congress appropriated $1.2 billion for what is called *Pigford II,* the second part of the case

Under the consent decree, an eligible recipient is an African American who (1) farmed or attempted to farm between January 1, 1981, and December 31, 1996, (2)

applied to USDA for farm credit or program benefits and believes that he or she was discriminated against by the USDA on the basis of race, and (3) made a complaint against the USDA on or before July 1, 1997. The consent decree set up a system for notice, claims submission, consideration, and review that involved a facilitator, arbitrator, adjudicator, and monitor, all with assigned responsibilities. The funds to pay the costs of the settlement (including legal fees) come from the Judgment Fund operated by the Department of the Treasury, not from USDA accounts or appropriations.

The lawsuit was filed in 1997 by Timothy Pigford, who was joined by 400 additional African-American farmer plaintiffs. Dan Glickman, the Secretary of Agriculture, was the nominal defendant. The allegations were that the USDA treated black farmers unfairly when deciding to allocate price support loans, disaster payments, "farm ownership" loans, and operating loans, and that the USDA had failed to process subsequent complaints about racial discrimination.

After the lawsuit was filed, Pigford requested blanket mediation to cover what was thought to be about 2,000 farmers who may have been discriminated against, but the U.S. Department of Justice opposed the mediation, saying that each case had to be investigated separately. As the case moved toward trial, the presiding judge certified as a class all black farmers who filed discrimination complaints against the USDA between 1983 and 1997.

The Pigford consent decree established a two-track dispute resolution mechanism for those seeking relief. The most widely used option was called "Track A" which could provide a monetary settlement of $50,000 plus relief in the form of loan forgiveness and offsets of tax liability. Track A claimants had to present substantial evidence (i.e., a reasonable basis for finding that discrimination happened) that: claimant owned or leased, or attempted to own or lease, farm land; claimant applied for a specific credit transaction at a USDA county office during the applicable period; the loan was denied, provided late, approved for a lesser amount than requested, encumbered by restrictive conditions, or USDA failed to provide appropriate loan service, and such treatment was less favorable than that accorded specifically identified, similarly situated white farmers; and the USDA's treatment of the loan application led to economic damage to the class member.

Alternatively, affected farmers could follow the "Track B" process. Track B claimants had to prove their claims and actual damages by a preponderance of the evidence (i.e., it is more likely than not that their claims are valid). The documentation to support such a claim and the amount of relief are reviewed by a third party arbitrator, who makes a binding decision. The consent decree also provided injunctive relief, primarily in the form of priority consideration for loans and purchases, and technical assistance in filling out forms. Finally, plaintiffs were permitted to withdraw from the class and pursue their individual cases in federal court or through the USDA administrative process.

This settlement was approved on April 14, 1999, by Judge Paul L. Friedman of the U.S. District Court for the District of Columbia.

Originally, claimants were to have filed within 180 days of the consent decree. Late claims were accepted for an additional year afterwards, if they could show extraordinary circumstances that prevented them from filing on time.

Far beyond the anticipated 2,000 affected farmers, 22,505 "Track A" applications were heard and decided upon, of which 13,348 (59%) were approved. US$995 million had been disbursed or credited to the "Track A" applicants as of January 2009, including US$760 million disbursed as US$50,000 cash awards. Fewer than 200 farmers opted for the "Track B" process. This was reportedly the largest federal settlement for civil rights violations to date.

Beyond those applications that were heard and decided upon, about 70,000 petitions were filed late and were not allowed to proceed. Some have argued that the notice program was defective, and others blamed the farmers' attorneys for "the inadequate notice and overall mismanagement of the settlement agreement". A provision in the 2008 farm bill essentially allowed a re-hearing in civil court for any claimant whose claim had been denied without a decision that had been based on its merits.

The largest compensation as of July 2010, from the first part of the Pigford case, was the $13 million paid to the members of the defunct collective farm New Communities of Southwest Georgia in 2009; their attorney said that the value of the land of their former 6,000-acre farm was likely worth $9 million alone.

Black Farmers and Agriculturalist Association filed a twenty and a half billion dollar class action lawsuit against the USDA for the same practices, alleging racially discriminatory practices between 1997 and 2004. The lawsuit was dismissed when the BFAA failed to show it had standing to bring the suit.

Legislative language was added to the 2008 Farm Bill to enable more farmers to bring suit and to authorize the government to negotiate additional monies for settlement. In 2010, the Administration had negotiated settlement for an additional $1.2 billion for such claims in what is known as *Pigford II*. Congress appropriated the money for the settlement later that year.

Miss Shirley Sherrod who later became an employee of the USDA whose father was murdered by a White man who was never prosecuted was now being burden with another racist empire. Namely the state of Georgia, United States Department of Agriculture and Governor Lester Maddox. Over 6000 acre was slowly and systematic being stolen from African American farmer by the USDA and the state of Georgia. Shirley Sherrod was the key person is creating what was often referred to as the African American utopia in the midst of a Georgia White farming community. The Black farmer was slowly going under with the help of the USDA and the power that be. To add insult to injury Governor Lester Maddox, referred to Black Farmers as Sharecropper City. Maddox stereo typical statement was to insinuate that Black Farmers should be under the control of White Farmers. The Black farmers plead with Governor Maddox to sign a grant to help keep their farms afloat but he refused preferring to see them fail. When they applied through the Farmers Home Administration for help they were given the run-around or given partial funding late in the crop season to delay planting and harvesting and to help insure that the farms would eventually fail. The USDA which was run by all Whites and administer the vast majority of farmer loans gave little to no priority to African American applicants. It took three times as long on the average to process loans for Black farmers as it did for White farmer. Under the President Reagan the USDA civil rights division was literally non existent which meant that most complaints of discrimination went into the trash can or thrown in a file drawer and forgotten.

The Black farmers were systematical and strategically targeted to be eliminated by both the state and federal government. After months and years of intimidation, harassment and bullying many of the farmer simply gave up to the pressure, realizing that all of their efforts were futile. The land was sold to White businessmen and later turned into subdivisions.

Miss Sherrod later that same year after new communities were built in the heart of a farm community once owned by African Americans was given the task of helping a White couple Eloise and Roger Spooner save their farm. The USDA had gained the dubious honor of being called the last plantation. She tells the story many years later in what became a very controversial speech. Sherrod worked for a nonprofit organization that helped farmers who were in danger of losing their farm. The Spooners were a White couple assigned to Miss. Sherrod. Sherrod made a speech which she admits that the idea of helping a White couple to save their farm after seeing so many Black farmers being ignored and forced into foreclosure didn't set well with Sherrod. Sherrod also state that after much soul searching that she felt compelled to help the Spooners and became close friends with them. This experience caused a pivotal change in Sherrod's life and her view of race; she learned to look beyond skin color and sought to work with all people who needed her help and expertise to save their farms.

It must have seemed ironic then, or perhaps even redemptive, for Sherrod when she was hired by the USDA in May 2009. The system she had battled for decades had chosen her to lead its Office of Rural Development in Georgia. "We're very proud of her and were delighted when she got the job at USDA," says Starry Krueger, president of the Rural Development Leadership Network, whose mission includes helping people living in poor rural areas earn advanced degrees and where Sherrod was a board member. The official White House announcement of Sherrod's appointment but did not mention her involvement in the class-action lawsuit.) It must have seemed even more ironic, and certainly cruel, when she was hastily sacked after a conservative blogger touted a short clip of her speech about the Spooners cut to make it seem as though she had proudly denied them help in an instance of reverse discrimination. This assination of her character was corrected much faster once the full context of Sherrod's parable about the Spooners became available, President Obama and Agriculture Secretary Tom Vilsack both personally apologized to Sherrod. She has been offered a new job and is considering whether to accept it. (Attempts to reach Sherrod Thursday were unsuccessful.) The White House has insisted it had nothing to do with the decision making process before the firing, which might have stung Sherrod almost as much as the firing itself. After all, as a Senator Obama had championed the black farmers' lawsuit against the USDA.

Accompanied by Republican Senator Chuck Grassley of Iowa, Obama introduced legislation to reopen the case (that was initially settled in 1999) to allow more black farmers to join and to provide more funding to settle claims. The legislative language was added to the Farm Bill passed in 2008 and its inclusion led to a second Administration-negotiated settlement in February of this year for $1.15 billion. Yet the money to actually fund that settlement must be approved by Congress, and so far the House and Senate have only been able to vote for it as part of different pieces of legislation. The money will not be appropriated unless both chambers vote on a single bill that includes the funding.

John Boyd, a Virginia farmer and founder and president of the National Black Farmers Association, told CNN in May he believes Obama is not pushing Congress hard enough to appropriate the money. He says the Administration is fearful of appearing to favor blacks and black causes over others, criticism that has been lobbed at the White House in recent days because of Sherrod's abrupt and misguided firing. Of the $1.15 billion funding request awaiting congressional action, Boyd has said, "I do think the Administration doesn't take it head-on because it is solely a black issue." On Thursday, with his hay growing and his soybeans already planted back in Virginia, Boyd was on Capitol Hill, lobbying Congress to approve the appropriation. He has already received what he describes as a "sizeable" settlement and continues the effort on behalf of others. He has organized protests in front of the USDA building in Washington to draw attention to his cause, and had hoped the legislative language required could be passed this week as an add-on to the unemployment bill. It was not. "We continue to push because so many black farmers have been treated so badly by the government," said Boyd.

African Americans and other minorities find it difficult if not almost impossible for any ethnic group to fulfill the American dream when it has built in vices to stop them. Soon the American dream simply becomes an illusion that many give up on and accept the crumbs from the "master table" and defeat. I have seen this scene play over and over all of my life and am as we speak in a dog fight for my survival. I thank God for the relationship that I have with him through my belief in Jesus Christ which sustain me in every walk of life.

Many terrorist have been born out of the abuses that they suffered at the hand of the legal systems. Seeing no other way or no fairness or justice they have instead choose to arm themselves and make a violent statement. I found the following statement fit my attitude perfectly and I recite it often to remind myself who I am and whose I am and who fights my battles.

Satan cannot defeat me; people cannot disillusion me; weather cannot worry me; sickness cannot stop me; government cannot silence me; and hell cannot handle me. I AM A CHILD OF THE ALMIGHTY GOD.

Reparations Indemnity For Slavery

Reparations was a proposal that some type of compensation should be provided to the descendants of enslaved people in the United States in consideration of the coerced and uncompensated labor their ancestors performed over centuries. This compensation has been proposed in a variety of forms, from individual monetary payments to land-based compensation schemes related to independence. The idea remains highly controversial and no broad consensus exists as to how it could be implemented. There have been similar calls for reparations from some

Caribbean countries and elsewhere in the African diaspora, and some African countries have called for reparations to their states for the loss of their population.

The arguments surrounding reparations are based on the formal discussion about many different reparations and actual land reparations received by African-Americans which were later taken away. In 1865, after the Confederate States of America were defeated in the American Civil War, General William Tecumseh Sherman issued Special Field Orders, No 15 to both "assure the harmony of action in the area of operations" and to solve problems caused by the masses of freed slaves, a temporary plan granting each freed family forty acres of tillable land in the sea islands and around Charleston, South Carolina for the exclusive use of black people who had been enslaved. The army also had a number of unneeded mules which were given to settlers. Around 40,000 freed slaves were settled on 400,000 acres (1,600 km²) in Georgia and South Carolina. However, President Andrew Johnson reversed the order after Lincoln was assassinated and the land was returned to its previous owners. In 1867, Thaddeus Stevens sponsored a bill for the redistribution of land to African Americans, but it was not passed.

Reconstruction came to an end in 1877 without the issue of reparations having been addressed. Thereafter, a deliberate movement of regression and oppression arose in southern states. Jim Crow Laws passed in some southeastern states to reinforce the existing inequality that slavery had produced. In addition white extremist organizations such as the Ku Klux Klan engaged in a massive campaign of intimidation throughout the Southeast in order to keep African Americans in their prescribed social place. For decades this assumed inequality and injustice was ruled on in court decisions and debated in public discourse.

Reparation for slavery in what is now the United States is a complicated issue. Any proposal for reparations must take into account the role of the, then relatively newly formed, United States government in importation and enslavement of Africans and that of the older and established European countries that created the colonies in which slavery was legal; as well as their efforts to stop the trade in slaves. It must also considered if and how much modern Americans have benefited from the importation and enslavement of Africans since the end of the slave trade in 1865. Profit from slavery was not limited to a particular region: New England merchants profited from the importation of slaves, while Southern planters profited from the continued enslavement of Africans. In a 2007 column in The New York Times, historian Eric Foner writes:

> In the Colonial era, Southern planters regularly purchased imported slaves, and merchants in New York and New England profited handsomely from the trade. The American Revolution threw the slave trade and slavery itself into crisis. In the run-up to war, Congress banned the importation of slaves as part of a broader nonimportation policy. During the War of Independence, tens of thousands of slaves escaped to British lines. Many accompanied the British out of the country when peace arrived.
>
> Inspired by the ideals of the Revolution, most of the newly independent American states banned the slave trade. But importation resumed to South Carolina and Georgia, which had been occupied by the British during the war and lost the largest number of slaves.
>
> The slave trade was a major source of disagreement at the Constitutional Convention of 1787. South Carolina's delegates were determined to protect slavery, and they had a powerful impact on the final document. They originated the three fifths clause (giving the South extra representation in Congress by counting part of its slave

population) and threatened disunion if the slave trade were banned, as other states demanded. The result was a compromise barring Congress from prohibiting the importation of slaves until 1808. Some Anti-Federalists, as opponents of ratification were called, cited the slave trade clause as a reason why the Constitution should be rejected, claiming it brought shame upon the new nation.

As slavery expanded into the Deep South, a flourishing internal slave trade replaced importation from Africa. Between 1808 and 1860, the economies of older states like Virginia came increasingly to rely on the sale of slaves to the cotton fields of Alabama, Mississippi and Louisiana. But demand far outstripped supply, and the price of slaves rose inexorably, placing ownership outside the reach of poorer Southerners.

Some proposals have called for direct payments from the U.S. government. One such proposal delivered in the McComick Convention Center conference room for the first National Reparations Convention by Howshua Amariel, a Chicago social activist, would require the federal government to make reparations to proven descendants of slaves. In addition, Amariel stated "For those blacks who wish to remain in America, they should receive reparations in the form of free education, free medical, free legal and free financial aid for 50 years with no taxes levied," and "For those desiring to leave America, every black person would receive a million dollars or more, backed by gold, in reparation." At the convention Amariel's proposal received approval from the 100 or so participants, nevertheless the question of who would receive such payments, who should pay them and in what amount, has remained highly controversial, since the United States Census does not track descent from slaves or slave owners and relies on selfreported racial categories.

Various estimates have been given if such payments were to be made. Harper Magazine has created an estimate that the total of reparations due is over 100 trillion dollars, based on 222,505,049 hours of forced labor between 1619 and 1865, with a compounded interest of 6%. Should all or part of this amount be paid to the descendants of slaves in the United States, the current U.S. government would only pay a fraction of that cost, over 40 trillion dollars, since it has been in existence only since 1789. There was never really an intent to fund this project. But it was a good political football to toss around to get a few moral points in the polls. Many accountant and statisticians were hired by congress to do millions of dollars of research into the possibility of reparation. These are ideal situations that many of the conservative politicians can use to reward that donors. They can request that hundreds of thousands of dollar be spent to consider the feasibility of paying for reparation. Some large firms may donate thousand and even hundreds of thousands of dollars to help get a friend elected. Of course the donors expect something in return for their donations. Big business look at making large campaign contributions as an investment and as with all investments by large corporation they expect a large return on their investments. Usually this is done in the form of contracts and grants given out by the federal government. The United States spend hundreds of millions of dollars on contracts and consultant contracts. This is a legal way to repay friends for their campaign contribution. Many of these contractors do little to nothing and receive hugh check every month. While many so call conservative complained of welfare recipients get a couple of hundred dollars per month the truth is those checks are a drop in the bucket compared to the multi-millions the government spends on consultant contracts. Many on which are simply kickbacks for campaign contributions.

The Rev. M.J. Divine, better known as Father Divine, was a well known activist with a national reputation of making firm stands. He was one of the earliest leaders to clearly argue for retroactive compensation as reparation for slavery. This message was spread over the world by a publication known as Peace Mission. Father Divine issued a Peace stamp on July 28, 1951 displaying the word "PEACE." Father Divine wanted all nations and people who were guilty of oppression and suppression to pay

African slaves and their descendants for all uncompensated servitude and for all unjust compensation, whereby they have been unjustly derived of compensation on the account of previous conditions of servitude and the present conditions of servitude

This is to be accomplished in the defense of all other underprivileged subjects and must be paid retroactive up-to-date. On July 30, 2008, the United States House of Representative One additional problem is that the governments in power in the 17th and 18th centuries in Europe are not still in power now. France, for example, has gone through several forms of government since it was last a colonial power in North America. It would be difficult, if not impossible, to hold the current French government liable for the enslavement of Africans that previous governments encouraged and benefited from between the 17th century up to the Louisiana Purchase in 1803. However, France can be held liable to Haiti, who won its independence from France in 1804, but the Haitians were victimized, enslaved, and imprisoned until slavery was abolished there by the French in 1848.

Professor Henry Gates suggest that the African nations must accept their role and responsibility in providing their share of the cost. The full cost of slavery reparations prior to 1776 would be borne by the governments of the European countries Spain, the United Kingdom, and France) who governed North America at that time. It is also liable to all French speaking countries in Africa. There are no indications that African governments will be expected to take part in any future reparation rounds. West African governments, in particular Nigeria, have become wealthier in recent years due to oil production and could be well placed to compensate descendants of slaves as a result of collusion and organization by traditional tribal leaders in the selling and exporting of their own people. Private institutions and corporations were also involved in slavery. On March 8, 2000, Reuters News Service reported that Deadria Farmer-Paellmann, a law school graduate, initiated a one-woman campaign making a historic demand for restitution and apologies from modern companies that played a direct role in enslaving Africans. Aetna Inc. was her first target because of their practice of writing life insurance policies on the lives of enslaved Africans with slave owners as the beneficiaries. In response to Farmer-Paellmann's demand, Aetna Inc. issued a public apology, and the "corporate restitution movement" was born.

Nine lawsuits were filed by the year 2002 around the country coordinated by Farmer-Paellmann and the Restitution Study Group—a New York non-profit. The litigation included 20 plaintiffs demanding restitution from 20 companies from the banking, insurance, textile, railroad, and tobacco industries. The cases were consolidated under 28 U.S.C. 1407 to Multidistrict litigation in the United States District Court for the Northern District of Illinois. The district court dismissed the lawsuits with prejudice, and the claimants appealed to the United States Court of Appeals for the Seventh Circuit. On December 13, 2006, that Court, in an opinion written by Judge Richard Posner, modified the district court's judgment to be a dismissal *without* prejudice, affirmed the majority of the district court's judgment, and reversed the portion of the district court's judgment dismissing the plaintiffs' consumer protection claims, remanding the case for further proceedings consistent with its opinion. Thus, the plaintiffs may bring the lawsuit again, but must clear considerable procedural and substantive hurdles first:

If one or more of the defendants violated a state law by transporting slaves in 1850, and the plaintiffs can establish standing to sue, prove the violation despite its antiquity, establish that the law was intended to provide a remedy (either directly or by providing the basis for a common law action for conspiracy, conversion, or restitution) to lawfully enslaved persons or their descendants, identify their ancestors, quantify damages incurred, and persuade the court to toll the statute of limitations, there would be no further obstacle to the grant of relief.

October 2000, California passed a Slavery Era Disclosure Law requiring insurance companies doing business there to report on their role in slavery. The disclosure legislation, introduced by Senator Tom Hayden, is the prototype for similar laws passed in 12 states around the United States.

The NAACP has called for more of such legislation at local and corporate levels. It quotes Dennis C. Hayes, CEO of the NAACP, as saying, "Absolutely, we will be pursuing reparations from companies that have historical ties to slavery and engaging all parties to come to the table." Brown University, whose namesake family was involved in the slave trade, has also established a committee to explore the issue of reparations. In February 2007, Brown University announced a set of responses to its Steering Committee on Slavery and Justice. While in 1995 the Southern Baptist Convention apologized for the "sins" of racism, including slavery.

In December 2005, a boycott was called by a coalition of reparations groups under the sponsorship of the Restitution Study Group. The boycott targets the student loan products of banks deemed complicit in slavery—particularly those identified in the Farmer-Paellmann litigation. As part of the boycott students are asked to choose from other banks to finance their student loans." In 2005, JP Morgan Chase and Wachovia both apologized for their connections to slavery. A number of supporters for reparations advocate that compensation should be in the form of community rehabilitation and not payments to individual descendants.

Wealth Accumulation

In 2008 the American Humanist Association published an article which argued that if emancipated slaves had been allowed to possess and retain the profits of their labor, their descendants might now control a much larger share of American social and monetary wealth. Not only did the freedmen and -women not receive a share of these profits, but they were stripped of the small amounts of compensation paid to some of them during Reconstruction. The wealth of the United States, they say, was greatly enhanced by the exploitation of Black slave labor. According to this view, reparations would be valuable primarily as a way of correcting modern economic imbalance. The US Department of Commerce has calculated that in modern US dollars calculated for inflation and interest, slavery generated trillions of dollars for the US economy.

Precedents

During the Reagan administration almost anything that had to do with the civil rights of African American was considered irrelevant. Under the Civil Liberties Act of 1988, signed into law by President Ronald Reagan, the U.S. government apologized for Japanese American internment during World War II and provided reparations of $20,000 to each survivor, to compensate for loss of property and liberty during that period. For many years, Native American tribes have received compensation for lands ceded to the United States by them in various treaties. Other countries have also opted to pay reparations for past grievances, such as the German government making reparations to Jew and survivors and descendants of the Holocaust.

Arguments against reparations

One of the principal argument against reparations is that their cost would not be imposed upon the perpetrators of slavery who were a very small percentage of society with 4.8% of southern whites (only 1.4% of all whites in the country), nor confined to those who can be shown to be the specific indirect beneficiaries of slavery, but would simply be indiscriminately borne by taxpayers.

Those making this argument often add that the descendants of white abolitionists and soldiers in the Union Army might be taxed to fund reparations despite the sacrifices their ancestors already made to end slavery.

In the case of Public Lands, European colonizers killed or relocated. Many Southeastern Native American tribes. One argument against reparations is that in assigning public lands to African-Americans for the enslavement of their ancestors, a greater and further wrong would be committed against the Southeastern Native Americans who have ancestral claims and treaty rights to that same land.

In addition, several historians, such as João C. Curto, have made important contributions to the global understanding of the African side of the Atlantic Slave Trade. By arguing that African merchants determined the assemblage of trade goods accepted in exchange for slaves, many historians argue for African agency and ultimately a shared responsibility for the slave trade.

Finally, as documented in the book *Black Slave Owners*, by Larry Koger, slaves were bought and sold and used for purely financial reasons by blacks in the pre-Civil War era. Some of the slave owners were freed slaves who immediately began enslaving other blacks, creating the possibility that if reparations were paid, they could actually be paid to descendants of slave owners.

Victim Identification and levels of victimization

Finding the identity of actual descendants of slaves would be an enormous undertaking, because such descent is not simply identical with present racial self-identification. And levels of actual victimization would be impossible to identify; had freed slaves been given their recoverable damages, they may have followed different patterns of marriage and of reproduction, and in some cases would not have made their offspring the sole or even principal heirs to their estates. (Opponents of reparations refer to the lost wealth of slaves as "dissipated", not in the sense of simply having ceased to exist, but in the sense of being untraceable and transmitted elsewhere.

It has been argued that reparations for slavery cannot be justified on the basis that slave descendants are subjectively worse off as a result of slavery, because it has been suggested that they are better off than they would have been in Africa if the slave trade had never happened. The slave population in the US grew six-fold after the importation of slaves was ceased. In all other countries the slave population either did not increase or declined. This was because the treatment of slaves in the US was generally better than other countries and had very good - birth survival rates exceeded that of poor whites and was twice that of their native Africa. In addition, each state had laws against the abuse of slaves and many religious groups rigorously enforced them.

In "Up From Slavery," former slave Booker T. Washington wrote,

> I have long since ceased to cherish any spirit of bitterness against the Southern white people on account of the enslavement of my race. No one section of our country was wholly responsible for its introduction... Having once got its tentacles fastened on to the economic and social life of the Republic, it was no easy matter for the country to relieve itself of the institution. Then, when we rid ourselves of prejudice, or racial feeling, and look facts in the face, we must acknowledge that, notwithstanding the cruelty and moral wrong of slavery, the ten million Negroes inhabiting this

country, who themselves or whose ancestors went through the school of American slavery, are in a stronger and more hopeful condition, materially, intellectually, morally, and religiously, than is true of an equal number of black people in any other portion of the globe....This I say, not to justify slavery – on the other hand, I condemn it as an institution, as we all know that in America it was established for selfish and financial reasons, and not from a missionary motive – but to call attention to a fact, and to show how Providence so often uses men and institutions to accomplish a purpose. When persons ask me in these days how, in the midst of what sometimes seem hopelessly discouraging conditions, I can have such faith in the future of my race in this country, I remind them of the wilderness through which and out of which, a good Providence has already led us.

Conservative commentator David Horowitz writes,

The claim for reparations is premised on the false assumption that only whites have benefited from slavery. If slave labor created wealth for Americans, then obviously it has created wealth for black Americans as well, including the descendants of slaves. The GNP of black America is so large that it makes the African-American community the 10th most prosperous "nation" in the world. American blacks on average enjoy per capita income in the range of twenty to fifty times that of blacks living in any of the African nations from which they were taken. (From Ten Reasons Why Reparations for Black is a Bad Idea for Blacks and Racist Too.

Legal argument against reparations

Some legal experts argue the point to the fact that slavery was not illegal in the United States prior to the Thirteenth Amendment to the United States Constitution (ratified in 1865). Thus, there is no legal foundation for compensating the descendants of slaves for the crime against their ancestors when, in strictly legal terms, no crime was committed. Chattel slavery is now considered by many to be highly immoral in the United States, though it was perfectly legal at the time. However, opponents of this legal argument contend that such was the case in Nazi Germany, whereby the activities of the Nazis were legal under German law. Unlike slavery, the German activities were precedent by the Allied Powers following WWI, which could not rule against the German government. Due to lack of precedent, but could do so afterward following WWII on the basis of this established WWI precedent.

Many legal experts point to the fact that the current U.S. government did not exist prior to June 21, 1788 when the United States Constitution was ratified. Therefore, the U.S. government inherited the institution of slavery, and cannot be held legally liable for the enslavement of Africans by Europeans prior to that time. Figuring out who was enslaved by whom in order to fairly apply reparations from the U.S. government only to those who were enslaved under U.S. laws, would be an impossible task.

Some areas of the South had communities of freedman, such as existed in Savannah, Charleston and New Orleans, while in the North, for example, former slaves lived as freedman both before and after the creation of the United States in 1788. For example, in 1667 Dutch colonists freed some of their slaves and gave them property in what is now Manhattan. The descendants of Groote and Christina Manuell two of those freed slaves can trace their family's history as freedman back to the child of Groote and Christina, Nicolas Manuell, whom they consider their family's first freeborn African-American. In 1712, the British, then in control of New York, prohibited blacks from inheriting land, effectively ending property ownership for this family. While this is only one example out of thousands of enslaved persons, it does mean that not all slavery reparations can be determined by racial self-identification alone; reparations would have to include a determination of the free or slave status of one's African-American ancestors, as well as when and by whom they were enslaved and denied rights such as property ownership. Because of slavery, the original African heritage has been blended with the American experience, the same as it has been for generations of immigrants from other countries. For this reason, determining a "fair share" of reparations would be an impossible task.

The most effective legal argument against reparations for slavery from a legal (as opposed to a moral standpoint) is that the statute of limitations for filing lawsuits has long since passed. Thus, courts are prohibited from granting relief. This has been used effectively in several suits, including "In re African American Slave Descendants", which dismissed a high-profile suit against a number of businesses with ties to slavery. Perhaps the most cogent argument against reparations (though this is not a legal argument) is that few African-Americans are of "pure" African blood since the offspring of the original slaves were occasionally the progeny of Caucasian male masters (and a variety of White males) by means of rape, concubinage or threat and forcibly slave-breeding of African and Black female slaves.

Reparations could cause increased racism

Anti-reparations advocates argue reparations payments based on race alone would be perceived by nearly everyone as a monstrous injustice, embittering many, and inevitably setting back race relations. In this view, apologetic feelings some whites may hold because of slavery and past civil rights injustices would, to a significant extent, be replaced by anger. The anti-reparation advocates argue that reparation shouldn't be based on race alone without considering the fact that the injustice was based on race alone. One may question why does this group think that the most important consideration in the reparation movement is what some Whites think. Should Black continue to suffer injustice to pacify a small group of White antagonist? If giving Black people justice causes some whites to become racist or angry then their opinion shouldn't matter anyway. I don't believe for one minute that the majority of Whites share those views and those who do are probably the remnant of the old Jim Crow era.

The Libertarian Party, among other groups and individuals, has suggested that reparations would make racism worse: A renewed demand by African-Americans for slavery reparations should be rejected because such payments would only increase racial hostility.

A leading work against reparations is David Horowitz, *Uncivil Wars: The Controversy Over Reparations for Slavery* (2002). Other works that discuss problems with reparations, although they are sympathetic in some ways to it, include John Torpey, *Making Whole What Has Been Smashed: On Reparations Politics* (2006) and Alfred Brophy, *Reparations Pro and Con* (2006).

There is also a technical problem with identifying those who should be entitled to exemptions because of their ancestral opposition to Slavery. In particular, there was a significant AntiSlavery Resistance Movement among the German and Mexican Texans during the Civil War which effectively negated the gains from New Mexico by choking off supplies.

SOWING AND REAPING (TERRORISM)

A lot of the terrorism we face in America is a direct result of the way America has treated people of other countries. Colonialism required the use of cruel and dehumanizing tactics to establish influence over it's subjects. Laws were improvised to oppress and suppress the native populations. Penalties were imposed according to ethnicity, race and color of the violators. The native populations were excluded from being attorneys, legal staff, and court personal or serving on juries.

There was a scramble for Africa also known as the "race for Africa" was the rush or hurry for African territories by European powers. These European powers rushed for African territories due to several reasons. These causes can be categorized into economic, social, political and humanitarian/social reasons. Europe banded together to invade the African continent after which they began the process of partitioning. Partitioning is the process of dividing shares of African land among European powers.

Europeans were referred to as imperialist in their quest for Africa's land. Imperialism is a term used to refer to the economic and political domination or control of one country or nation by another one which has superior technology and is more economically advanced. Therefore, European imperialism had the dominating effects upon the economics and politics of other nations all over the world. Europe has for more than three centuries managed to extend its influence and imperialism into other continents such as the West Indies, Latin America, Asia, and Africa. Europe was able to influence these countries because of most of the European nations were relatively economically and militarily stronger that the countries they chose to invade and conquer on other continents. There was a need for raw material among the European nations due to it industrial revolution. Machinery increased production which increased the need for raw materials such as copper, palm oil, rubber, gold and cocoa. Africa was seen as a very good source for all of the raw materials needed for the industrial revolution. With this knowledge the European powers partitioned Africa in order to secure some territories to have unlimited access to these raw materials which could supply their industries in Europe.

With the help of machines during the Industrial Revolution, more goods were produced in the European Industries but the local consumption was the same. This meant that not all the good produced in Europe were locally sold and used in Europe. Therefore, European powers had to look for other areas where they could go and sell their surplus products. Africa was a suitable place for this mission. Africa was suitable because Africa did not have industries to produce these goods.

The industrial Revolution had made many European businessmen very rich by 1880. Many of these had accumulated surplus capital which they wanted to invest abroad for profit because profit had fallen in their respective countries due to the high cost of labor. Therefore, they believed that Africa could provide them with cheap labor. Thus, they started encouraging their home governments to acquire colonies in Africa

Before 1800, many European countries had allowed the formation of companies to promote overseas trade. Examples of these companies include the British Royal Niger Company in West Africa, the British South African company (B.S.A.C) in South Africa, the Imperial British East Africa and the Germany East African Company in Tanganyika. The second half of the 19th Century saw stiff competition among these companies. As a result these companies were forced to ask their home governments to take over certain African areas where they could enjoy the trade monopoly.

There was a need for a balance of power so after the Berlin Congress was held and the Russo-Turkish war of 1877-78 shortly thereafter. European nations realized that there was no power in Europe which was more powerful than the others. This meant that no country in Europe could expand its sphere within Europe without risking a major war. These powers therefore turned to Africa were there was no resistant.

Due to the rise of nationalism, many Europeans had developed strong pride and patriotism and loyalty for their countries. They wanted to promote the status of their countries' position in the world. The possession of a large overseas empire became a symbol of braveness. The more colonies a country had, the more powerful it was considered to be, or rather, considered it to be. France for example, when France was defeated in 1871, she lost her two provinces of Alsace and Lorraine to German, Hence, France turned to Africa for colonies were there was no resistance. Other Europeans obtained colonies for personal glory. King Leopold of Belgium acquired the Congo Free State and treated it as a personal farm. This encouraged other Europeans to acquired farms in Africa and do the same while using the native for slave laborer.

Other European nations obtain colonies in Africa so as to provide a source and base for troops. For example, France obtained Senegal and Britain obtained part of Senegal and South Africa. Africans from these territories were used to fight on their respective sides during the First World War.

Strategic Purposes

Other parts in Africa were obtained by European powers because of their strategic positions. Areas like Egypt, Morocco, Mozambique, Angola, and the Cape were obtained to control trade in times of peace and war. British interest in Egypt was the Suez Canal. This provides a faster sea route to India.

Social Reasons

One must understand that because of the new machines that were being used during the industrial revolution, that many people lost employment in Europe because it was the newly invented machines that were doing their work now. Because of the unemployment due to the Industrial Revolution, European countries seized colonies in Africa to settle their surplus unemployed population. Nigeria Rhodesia and Kenya were seized for this purpose.

The Spread of Christianity

The partition of Africa was due in part to this reasoning. Some Europeans decided to seize colonies in Africa so as to convert the Africans into Christianity. Although African was one of the first places that Christianity took root from the beginning of Christianity so there no need for this mission. The Bible plainly states in Act 2:10 that at the foundation of the Christian Church that nations of Africa were present. Christianity and civilizations were used throughout European history as an excuse to cover up greed and theft of third world countries. If the perpetrators told the public that they were invading Africa for the purpose of civilizing them and spreading Christianity then they were more likely to accept the murder, torture, robbery and rapes that followed the invasions. Missionaries and explorers opened up the interior of Africa. Their reports about the richness of Africa encouraged the scramble. It is the reports of the accounts of such missionaries and explorers like Dr. David Livingstone that pushed the European countries to have overseas possessions.

Many wealthy but sick European people found the climate in Africa was better for their illnesses, so many made Africa their home.

Proposal to End Slave Trade

Britain took the lead in fighting against slave trade by passing a law in 1807; in 1833 the British government again passed the Emancipation act by which slavery was abolished throughout the British Empire. Many European nations had done the same. However, slave trade continued and other methods had failed.

The Berlin Colonial Conference of 1884/85

European powers formed a collaboration called the Berlin Colonial Conference held in Berlin, Germany in 1884-85 at the invitation of Bismarck, the Chancellor of Germany. The aim of the meeting was to discuss the peaceful division and sharing of African territories amongst themselves. At the end of this conference, the Berlin Treaty was signed. It laid down the conditions by which the scramble and carnage was to be conducted.

The Europeans powers agreed that any power claiming any territory in Africa must not only notify other powers but must also effectively occupy that territory. It was this clause of effective occupation in their agreement that encouraged and pushed

European powers to partition the continent and to abolished in all the territories that the European countries occupied.

No African Chief was invited to this meeting or consulted about the whole process of dividing up. Soon after this meeting ended agents of many European powers started coming to African and began its reign of terror of forceful demarcate boundaries for their claims, which became known as colonies. Liberia and Abyssina (Ethiopia) survived the invasion and were left independent. Any tribes that rebel against these invading European powers were quickly massacred or it's leader tortured and coerced into submission.

The acquiring of territories by European powers was not always peaceful. They came into conflict over colonies with Britain and France. Earlier, the British and French government had been giving financial support to Egypt. In 1881, the Egyptians under Arabic Pasha led a rebellion against the foreign financial control. Pasha and his followers attacked all foreigners and their properties. Britain then asked France to jointly intervene in this issue but the later refused. Britain then sent her army and occupied Egypt by force. This occupation annoyed the French who left Egypt in anger. Britain declared Egypt a British protectorate in 1882. The continuous British occupation of Egypt created on going tension between Britain and France.

HOPELESS PEOPLE ARE DANGEROUS PEOPLE

Last night, I watched the Michael Brown story. Michael Brown was a young Black man that lived in Ferguson, Missouri.

Several months ago, as the news med reported; Michael Brown went into a small neighborhood store and took some cigars without paying for them and assaulted the owner. The police were called and a report made. As a White police officer patrolled the streets he noticed two Black men walking in the middle of the street. The officer alleges to have told the two men to get out of the street when he noticed cigars in the possession of one of the men. He recalled earlier that there was a report of a robbery of cigars from a store nearby. An argument ensued and the officer states that Michael Brown struck him in the face with his fist. According to the officer Michael Brown tried to take his gun and the gun discharged. The young Black man reportedly retreated and the officer pursued and fired more shots striking Michael Brown six times killing him. Ironically two of the fatal shots were to the head of Michael Brown. For months people protested, some peacefully and other not so peacefully. The prosecutor ordered a grand jury which returned a "no true bill" freeing the officer of any wrong doing. After the announcement fires and arson broke out destroying millions of dollars in property.

A prosecutor has the ability to get a "true bill" or a "no true bill" in almost any case. There is no other attorney to object to the evidence being given the grand jury. The prosecutor can chose to present the type of information he wants to give to the grand jury to get the desired outcome. The grand jury purpose is not to try the case but only to see If there is enough evidence to justify a trial. The prosecutor in the Michael Brown case decided to overwhelm the grand jury with so much information and witnesses as to try the case in the grand jury hearing which is not its' purpose at all. The fairness of the prosecutor had been questioned in pass cases similar to Michael Brown. The correct and ethical thing to do for the prosecution would have been to recuse (remove) himself from the case. Then have the attorney general appoint a special prosecutor to eliminate any appearance of impropriety.

Police in this country have a very difficult job. They must deal with the population that we as citizens often fear. They must be willing to put their life on the line. This is what a police officer signs up for when he puts on the badge and accepts the job.

Every time that I think that I am finish with this book project another story appears that I find that I must include in this book.

Eric Garner died in Tompkinsville neighborhood of Staten Island, New York, after a police officer put him in an apparent chokehold for about 19 seconds. This tactic is banned by the New York City Police Department. Garner was initially approached by officer Justin Damico on suspicion of selling "loosies," single cigarettes from packs without tax stamps.

After Garner expressed to the police that he was tired of being harassed and that he was not selling cigarettes, officers made the move to arrest Garner. Officer Daniel Panteleo, also on scene, put his arms around the much taller Garner's neck, applying an apparent chokehold shown in a video recording of the event, which has since gone viral. While lying face down on the sidewalk surrounded by four officer, Garner is heard repeatedly saying "I can't breathe," eleven times, he repeated this statement to the officers. Garner was pronounced dead approximately one hour later at the hospital.

The medical examiner concluded that Garner was killed by neck compression from the apparent chokehold, along with "the compression of his chest and prone position during physical restraint by police." Contributing factors include bronchial asthma, heart disease, obesity, and hypertensive and cardiovascular problems.

Two of the police officers were stripped of their service guns and badge and placed on desk duty. On December 3, 2014 a grand jury decided not to indict officer Pantaleo. This decision by the grand jury stirred public protest and rallies in New York and in many cities across America. A large segment of the American public believes these act by police officers are brutal and unnecessary. Attorney General Eric Holder announced that the Justice Department would launch an "independent, thorough, fair, and expeditious" civil rights investigation into Garner's death.

Eric Garner had been employed as horticulturist at the New York City Department of Parks and Recreation, Garner at 6'3" inches weighed about 350 pounds and was 43 years old African American man. His friends described him as a neighborhood peacemaker; and as a generous, congenial person. Garner was the father of six children. He had previously been arrested and was out on bail for selling untaxed cigarettes, driving without a license, marijuana possession, and false impersonation. Garner criminal record includes more than thirty arrest dating back to 1980 on charges such as assault, resisting arrest, grand larceny. An official said the charges include multiple incidents in which he was arrested for selling unlicensed cigarettes.

Officer Daniel Pantaleo

Daniel Panteleo is a white New York City Police Department officer who was, at the time of Garner's death, age 29 and living in Eltingville, Staten Island. Pataleo's father was a New York City Fire Department firefighter, and his uncle was a NYPD officer. He graduated from Monsignor Farrell High School and received a bachelor's degree from College of Staten Island. He joined the NYPD in 2006. Pantaleo was the subject of two civil rights lawsuits in 2013 where plaintiffs accused Pantaleo of falsely arresting them and abusing them. In one cases Pantaleo and other officers ordered two black men to strip naked on the street for a search and the charges against the men was dismissed.

Attorney General Eric Holder states that the Department of Justice was "closely monitoring investigation into Garner's death.

Both president George Bush and Obama addressed the grand jury's decision by making a speech, stating that Garner's death and the legal outcome of it is an "American problem. George W. Bush said that he found the verdict "hard to understand" and "very sad" in an interview.

The NYPD Police Commissioner William Bratton order and extensive review of the police training procedures specifically focusing on the appropriate amount of force that can be used while detaining a suspect. The leader of the police union Patrolmen's

Benevolent Association challenged the claim that a chokehold was used. Police union officials as well as officer Pantaleo's lawyer argued that Pantaleo did not use a takedown move taught by the police department because Garner was resisting arrest.

Garner's daughter Erica believes that it was pride and not racism that led to the officer choking her father to death.

Tamir Rice

Tamir Rice was a 12 year old boy living in Cleveland Ohio who was shot by police officer. The police officers allege that Tamir refused to put down a pellet pistol when ordered by police.

The attorney for the family states that Tamir Rice went to the park with friends one Saturday afternoon, but he did not know the details of what led to the shooting. Witnesses reported a male was in the playground area waving a gun and pointing it at people. A man called 911 and told dispatchers the boy was on a swing set and pointing a pistol that was "probably fake" and scaring everyone. The caller said the boy was pulling the gun in and out of his pants. "I don't know if it's real or not," the caller said. Jeff Follmer, president of the Cleveland Police Patrolmen's Association, said the officers were not told that the caller thought the gun might be fake. Follmer said the officer called to the playground outside a city recreation center saw the pistol sitting on a table or bench, and watched the boy grab it and put it in his waistband. Police said after officers arrived, they told him to raise his hands, an order the child allegedly did not follow.

"The young man had the weapon in his waistband. He pulled the weapon out. One of our officers fired two shots, striking the young man, "Deputy Chief Ed Tomba with the Cleveland Police Department told WOIO television. The boy had an Airsoft replica gun that had the orange safety indicator removed police said.

When Police Don't Police

Over a week ago we watched the marvel of technology again expose systematic corruption of persons sworn to serve and protect the citizens of this great country. I am speaking of the police officer who murdered an unarmed man. This officer was caught on video committing murder by shooting an unarmed citizen multiple times in the back. This same officer had been reported numerous times prior to this incident to his superiors yet nothing was done about his conduct. When the police refuse to police it's rank it often leads to overly aggressive police officer getting further and further out of control until something like this happens.

Police work is very demanding and requires a lot of endurance and self-control. When officer begin to cross that line of self-control their departments should step in and begin some type of intervention. The intervention should include counseling, relaxation therapy, re- training and whatever else may be necessary to ensure public safety. Sometimes officers need a case management approach with close monitoring.

Complaints by citizens against police should always be taken seriously. When police supervisors send a message to police officers that complaints will be ignored, it opens the door for abuse and misconduct and in this case murder. Too often police supervisors simply look the other way when complaints are filed unless of course the media gets involved. This is usually when someone has been killed or seriously injured in a run in with the police.

When a man is murdered on a misdemeanor traffic stop it is time for major changes in the way police officers are trained and supervised. The irony is that the vast majority of victims of unprovoked murders by police officers are African Americans. For some reason and too often it seems that Black men's lives don't matter. This was obvious the sentiment of the officer who murdered the Black man running from him. The officer was recording laughing standing over the man's body that he had just murder. He seemed to have no emotional feelings whatsoever of the brutal act of murder that he had just committed. His attitude reminds me of a group of guys at a deer hunt after someone had just shoot a big buck.

It is such a sad testimony when we have to relive these type of incidents on a weekly basis of police murder and brutality.

COMMUNITY POLICING

There are far too many needless deaths of Black men killed by police as well as other Black men. One way to help curb these killing by police is to have community policing. Get the police out of the cars and on bicycles and walking the neighborhoods. This will create a more friendly relationship between the neighborhoods and the police. When people talk to each other they come to know each other and are less likely to distrust and hate each other. When people began to call each other by name, share their joy and disappointments with each other a completely different atmosphere evolves. Special forces troops are taught that if they are captured to try to create a dialogue with the enemy so that the enemy will began to see you as a person and not just a combatant to be destroyed. This same philosophy can be applied to the adversarial relationship that exist between the police and minorities in many inner cities and proverty stricken areas in American. Change begins with a sincere desire and love for one's fellow citizens. Our cities are becoming hot beds that are about to erupt at any given time. These hot beds put our police and inner city citizens in great danger. Not only does the unhealthy climate that is produced by the negative relationships between inner city minorities and police do great social and emotion harm but also affects the economy in a very negative fashion.

Many cities in America are already suffering from economic hardships and budgets that cannot be balanced. When the riots come it cause hundreds of millions of dollars in damages. A large number of America's industrial cities are on the verge of bankruptcy due to the loss of businesses and industries because a vast number of our fortune 500 companies send their work off shore to places like China, Mexico and India and get huge tax deductions at the expense of the working middle class who too often are the working poor.

Eric Garner did not deserve to be murdered as he was by police officer. The officer over reacted and when Eric Garner capitulated the threat no longer exist. The "choke hold" should had stopped when he said, "I can't breathe." The officers should have been brought to trial for the murder of Eric Garner.

When people feel that they are excluded and disenfranchised violence and mayhem is the results. Blacks are not represented in law enforcement or any major governing body in Ferguson. Some of the unrepresentation is because only thirteen percent of the African American Community vote. Many don't believe that their vote matter; others are just unconcern due to years of frustration and disappointment. We must address the issues of injustice and racism that are still alive and well in America.

As a Black man who has been a police officer and a victim of injustice by the legal system it makes it very difficult to have any confidence or trust in courts or law enforcement. Considering the fact that I hold a Master Degree several licenses and certifications and yes I have been a victim of the Louisiana legal system that feel comfortable in prosecuting, lying and trumping up false charges on Black man without reservation. Why would anyone believe that this legal system would do anything different to a blue collar worker that is less educated and informed minority person. There is a lot of distrust in the minority community of the legal system and rightfully so. We all must understand that justice denied anyone is justice denied everyone.

CONCLUSION:

A pastor by the name of Niemoller was placed in a concentration camp during the holocaust. He wrote about the cowardice of the German society as they watched the Nazi terrorize and dismantle their society group by group. Pastor Niemoller writes:

"First they came for the Socialist, and I did not speak out, because I was not a Socialist. Then they came for the Trade Unionists, and I did not speak out, because I was not a Trade Unionist. Then they came for the Jews, and I did not speak out, because I was not a Jew. Then they came for me; and there was no one left to speak for me."

The truth of the matter is that America's legal system is a terrible system. But the good news is the other societies of the world are so much worse. We here in the United States not only have the right but the duty to speak out against injustices. Freedom is not something that will be given to you it is something you must take. I got a letter from the U.S. Justice Department about a month after I got my copyright for this book. I assume this was an attempt to frighten me into not publishing this book; but to the contrary it only strengthen my commitment to expose injustices. motivated me even more. It cost a lot to stand up for righteousness but one pays so much more when they don't.

We who love this country are always seeking how to make this country a better place. One should never allow anything or anyone to deprive them of their free speech, life, liberty nor their pursuit of happiness. Not only is that your constitutional right but first and foremost it is your God given right. Never allow fear to be your motivator; fear no man only fear him who has the power to not only kill your body but cast your soul into hell, he's the one to fear. I pray that this book has been a blessing to you. I hope it has increased your knowledge and gave you the drive to pursue a better state and a better America. God bless you all.

COPYRIGHT 2015

ISBN 978-1-943276-90-5

All rights reserved. No part of this publication may be reproduced, stored in a retrieval system, or transmitted in any form or by any, means, electronic, mechanical, photocopying, recording, or otherwise. This book may not be reproduced, copied in any form or fashion without the written consent of the owner Donald Britton.

Contact information: Electronic Mail donaldbritt44@yahoo.com
Telephone (225) 774-3785 Facebook= DONALD BRITTON

THE BOOK

The author of this book documents with observations, personal experiences, and public records that the criminal justice system is not "blind" to race, gender, social class, economic status, social connections, place of residence nor the reputation of the defendant, the accuser, or the witnesses. Nor is the criminal justice system blind to the race, gender, and social status of the police, prosecutors, judges, jurors, or correctional officers and that discretionary justice often leads to injustice. In "American Justice System Uncovered" the author not only provides knowledge of the problems in the criminal justice system, but also solutions which serves as a source of motivation for public dialogue on how to elevate these problems in our system of justice or otherwise the need for reform and social change. This book will awaken you to many of the disparities in the American legal system and how you can help change them. Always remember that you are either part of the problem or part of the solution.

www.ingramcontent.com/pod-product-compliance
Lightning Source LLC
LaVergne TN
LVHW011934070526
838202LV00054B/4633